FUTURE SUSTAINABLE NEIGHBORHOOD
– A PRIMER

TONY BUCK

PLANET PUBLISHING

Pennsylvania, USA

DISCLAIMER

To the best of my knowledge and research, the information contained herein is accurate. Much of what is mentioned I have put into practice. Follow all safety protocols when using tools or working on a project.

When using tools or machinery, always take sufficient time and position your body and limbs behind a tool, blade, saw, or drill, etc.; this rule professionals always seek to obey.

Copyright ©2025
By Tony Buck
Pennsylvania, USA

www.tonybuck.com

All rights reserved. No portion of this book may be reproduced in any manner without written permission from the author.

ISBN 978-0-9646802-4-1

First Edition

786

Contents

PROLOGUE: Visit to a Future Sustainable Neighborhood   1
INTRODUCTION: Future Sustainable Neighborhood – A Primer   4
PART 1: THE WHATS?   6
HOUSEHOLD ENERGY: OVERVIEW OF SYSTEMS   6
Centralized Energy Sources   6
Renewable Energy is the People's Power   8
Soar Energy   8
First, Solar Photovoltaic Panels   8
Solar Hydronic Panels   10
Home-sized Wind Turbine   10
Community Energy Solutions   10
Personal Woodstove Energy   10
BELOW FROSTLINE PHENOMENON   11
Passive Space Cooling, Heating and Food Storage   11
NEGA-WATTS   13
NO NUCLEAR   15
EXTERIOR COOL/HEAT STRATEGY   15
SUMMER/WINTER SUN ANGLE PHENOMENON   15
Sun-penetrable Structures   16

RESILIENT LIFESTYLE   17
Reduce Expenses across the board   17
Transport   17
Join Community   18
Work   18
Home   18
Time Bank   18
Visioning   19
Place based awareness   19
Know Energy   19
More Actions   20
When Replacing Appliances   20
Energy Resilience Assessments   20
Renovating or Re-modeling   21
12inch (30cm) walls   21
Insulated Panel   21
Take Control   22

ORGANIC EDIBLE GARDENING LIFESTYLE   22
Herbs   31
Some Gardening Styles   33
Grow Food on Roofs   33
Wicking Planters   34
Closing The 'Anything Organic' Loop   36
Nature in the Garden   38
Trees in the FSN   39
Succession   41
SEEING NOT LOOKING – Soilnoia   43
RAINWATER HARVESTING   44
Rainwater Specs   44
GO DEEP FOR SUSTAINABLE ANSWERS   48
COMMUNITY   49
HEALTH   49
HUMAN WASTE   50
MISCELANIOUS   50
SEEING NOT LOOKING – Emergy   51
BUSINESS OPPORTUNITIES   51
The Household Economy   52
Ideas   54
Food System   54
Crafts/Products   54
Home-based Education   55
Services   55
Conclusion   56
ABOUT TIME AND LABOR   57
SEEING NOT LOOKING – Systems Thinking   57
PERMACULTURE   59
SEEING NOT LOOKING – MY 1500 CE., U.S. landscape muse   60
SEEING NOT LOOKING – It's Enough   61

PART 2: THE WHYS?   62
The Great Dilemma – A message from Nature   62
1. Two worlds: Mine and yours   63
2. Universal Basic Income   64
3. Reduce consumerism   65
4. Make planned obsolescence illegal   67
5. Make right-to-repair mandatory   67
6. Re-use, Reduce, Recycle, Upcycle, Clean-up   68

7   Discourage Fashion in all Products   69
8. Curtail Advertising   69
9. Revamp Financial System   70
10 Subsidize Income for: Farm Workers (farmers), School Teachers, Police, Healthcare Workers, Social Workers   70
11. De-commodify Food, Education, Healthcare   71
12. Re-localize the Food System Worldwide (Encourage locally sourced lifestyles)   72
13 Reduce Agricide, Increase Regenerative Agriculture Worldwide   74
14 Reduce Animal Food Consumption World-wide   75
15 Encourage Plant-based Eating   76
16. Re-skill for Home Cooking, Reduce Processed Food Intake   77
17. Revamp Public Education   78
18. 5 – 12 years old, Self-reliant, Systems Thinking Education   79
19. Champion All Renewable Energy, NOT Nuclear   80
20. Continue to Reduce Fossil Fuel Use   81
21. Conserve Energy, Insulation, smart design, etc.   82
22. Empower Women World-wide   82
23. Innovate Less Harmful Air Conditioning Systems.   83
24. Encourage Faith Communities to Get Involved   83
25. No expectations   85
Wrap Up   86
Further reading/resource   86
Index   87

PROLOGUE:
Visit to a future sustainable neighborhood

The first breath I took in this future neighborhood, the air had a fragrant quality that I didn't recognize. I could hear a person shout something, maybe a block away, it's much quieter than the world I left. There's certainly a smell of home cooking in the air. And there's a lot more plants of all sizes and description wherever I look. That's it! The air carries a mixture of fruit scents.

When I can see through the vegetation, the built environment has changed. Seems everyone has some kind of glass or see-thru plastic structure connected to the southerly facing side of their houses. (Because I'm in the northern hemisphere, if I'd been in the southern those would be on the north side of the house.) That encourages a longer food growing season in spring and fall, and in many places, greens grow all through the winter.

A lot of those walls are painted dark blue, reds and browns, probably to absorb more of the winter sun's heat. On that side of the houses, there's also a darker color of window blinds, for those who have them, probably for the same reason.

Wherever there's a flat roof, there's either a glow above it, suggesting a reflecting surface, or there's a low railing with what looks like, edible plants growing on the roof.

The gardens might look like plant chaos to some, but actually, I can see, it's very deliberate managed abundance.

There's strange configurations of gutters and downspouts connected around the buildings, suggesting people are making efforts at rainwater harvesting; maybe for their plantings, or household use and supplemental drinking water. Sky-water I call it, it's everywhere when there's no drought. Yes, I can see large tanks beautifully decorated and cleverly integrated into the landscaping. There must be a need to capture water when it's abundant.

Here and there, behind fences and hedgerows, I can hear the cluck of chickens. Almost all roofs have some configuration of solar voltaic or solar hydronic panels and what looks like miniature wind turbines, integrated into the roof design.

On the next block I can see workers retrofitting a house with a partial basement or cellar. Below the frost line in any country the earth is a constant 45-50 degrees Fahrenheit, 7-10 degrees Celsius. In the U.S., before electrification, this phenomenon was used to store vegetables for months in winter (root cellars), to prevent them from freezing. But now, in an ever-warming world, it's a great passive way to keep a cool room in summer. Houses with basements have become a premium.

Oh, here's a sign: Free extra compost, please take. That's nice, I sense many people have integrated an organic edible gardening lifestyle into their daily rounds. And there's a lot more people cycling, walking in the streets and pottering around in their gardens, and it's a week day. That suggests work-week hours have been reduced, probably due to robotics and AI in the workplace, and a reduction in consumerism from resources becoming strained to their limits. And 'transactions of decline,' ill-informed strategies instigated by politicians who misunderstood the complexity of the era.

Another sign: Jane and Charly's wood shop 9 to 5 week days. And a temporary sign: Surplus hemp cloth available at # 17. Sounds like working with fabric is popular again. What's this? It reads: Site of our new Hentrepreneur center, (Household entrepreneur). I notice it says 'our' center, not 'the' center, I sense a community spirit in this neighborhood.

There's graffiti on this building site, it says: Solve basic needs for everyone first. And another: Forget MTV, embrace MITP: Music In

The Park, every Saturday afternoon and evening.

Here and there are obelisk shaped structures about 2 meters or yards high, they are community-scale electric backup storage batteries for the grid, to facilitate solar and wind generated electricity. Their walls have become unofficial bulletin boards, posted with information about local services and objects for freecycle. Utility and communication cables now running under the ground, due to the frequency of extreme weather events.

In some neighborhoods the first small electric generating stations are being built, powered by the heat from thousands-of-feet-deep geothermal wells. Decentralization of the grid now being a priority for more security. (This had only been made possible recently because the majority of people finally understood how the fossil fuel industry had for years been one of the greatest impediments to alternative inventive progress.)

Most neighbors belong to the local Timeshare association. And every street has public benches where folks can rest or chat with a neighbor, with bicycle racks designed in.

I come across a small group of people filling in potholes in the road, one person from the public works department guiding a few neighborhood volunteers. This has become a standard arrangement in many municipalities in recent years. Looks like a local resident is bringing out some refreshment for them, I think I'll head over and see if I can get in on it! And, I drew and painted a mural of what I've described, but I'm sure there's still more to discover that isn't visible. So, let's explore these themes further....

INTRODUCTION
Future Sustainable Neighborhood– A Primer (FSN)

All the built-environment features I observed while imagining this future sustainable neighborhood, can be achieved today. Amory Lovins, co-founder of the Rocky Mountain Institute, said: "We don't need any novel technology, we need smarter design." I love that!

Many of the features require some capital outlay, but will add to the value of the property. Some, like the sun-penetrable structures(conservatory/sun-room additions), to extend food growing through almost all seasons, can be used for other lifestyle enhancements. Then, should the need arise, they are in place to serve you in a more urgent time. These basic-needs enhancements help us move toward more sustainable households, because, at present, most people in the modern industrialized countries, are frankly, sitting ducks, when it comes to infrastructure and supply chain disruptions.

I became aware of how fragile our modern construct was during the financial crash of 2008/9. Frankly, I was appalled that I was at the mercy of the greedy ghouls of Wall Street and that they could pull the rug out from under my life. And now, apart from deniers, there is of course climate change and an indefinite-food-crisis, simmering below the surface. Add up all the other Earth-System tipping points like: biodiversity loss, the need to phase down fossil fuels, the need to increase renewable energy sources exponentially, the need to protect against extreme weather events, and all that brings; the social and supply chain disruption from regional conflicts, the need to reduce consumerism – all known variously as the Poly, or Meta-crisis. So, I started thinking how to become, at least somewhat, more self-reliant and sustainable. It's very hard to be self-sufficient – where one needs no inputs from elsewhere – especially in the urban space, but we can aim for a confident level of self-reliance.

There are so many experts that I listen to and respect, who can run down the list of problems, but rarely does anyone suggest something concrete to do. I thought, maybe I can contribute to that, because I'm not siloed in a discipline, and have accumulated many skills during my life. So, one evening, I found myself imagining a visit to a future sustainable neighborhood, inspired by all the people I've read and listened to who are concerned about our future.

The ideas I'm sharing here have been influenced by the book, Just Enough, Lessons in living green from traditional Japan, by Azby Brown; and inspired by Rob Hopkins' work, co-founder of the Transition Town initiative. I'll also add, I completed a Permaculture Design Certificate in 2011, which helped me see the world in a more complete, connected way. So, I must thank David Holmgren and the late Bill Molison, the founders of Permaculture for their inspiration to.

Azby Brown wrote, "Sustainable society will come, because the alternative is no society at all. [...] However, we have nearly lost the race against time [...] our margin for avoiding unpleasantness has largely evaporated."

The first agriculture was labor intensive. The second, today's, is energy, machine and chemical intensive, very wasteful (subsidized) and toxic. Permaculture is design and information intensive, not just for agriculture, the Permaculture Principles can be applied to all we do. We can react to chaos, or design our future while we still have time and so much abundance.

There was a mini-rush from city to rural during the pandemic (plague) of the early 2020s. Mainly driven by claustrophobia, not sustainability. But with future disruption, not everyone can do that (including me), so we need to sustain-in-place. I've been doing much of this on my own one-tenth of an acre, urban property, and although not self-sufficient, there are improvements in my energy and daily needs. The edible plants I do grow yield more than I can eat, and so I share the harvest with neighbors and they share their biomass (garden 'waste' like leaves and grass clippings) with me, and that becomes the regenerative elements – compost – for "next year's groceries," as one of my neighbors calls it! Many commercial fertilizers are derived from fossil fuel and I'm trying to reduce my dependence on those.

Now, the irony is, we have to build the infrastructure needed to thrive, and that means a little more development to get us to where we need to be. And it does cost money. I have little surplus in that area, but those of us without cash must 'do it ourselves.' Because of my skill base, I accomplish this with my own labor and ability to adapt and repurpose supplies from used products, or score some at a local building supply auction. So, there is no excuse if you are able-bodied – get reskilled and start designing, planning and making. The next phase of the adventure: solving our discombobulated future/present. So, ideally, we'll create sustainable neighborhoods, because we're going to need trusted community connections. Can YouTube help us? It could, if the internet stays up and running.

This tome is an attempt to alert us to the urgency and suggest some of the elements we need to future-thrive. Feel free to have positive imaginings and innovate, improve and be part of this collective effort. The future may be here sooner than we think.

A mention on fossil fuels: oil, natural gas and coal. It turns out there are no energy transitions! What? When a replacement energy source emerges and takes precedent, the old sources are still used and may even increase in use by some unintended consequence, (we must always keep an eye out for these). E.g., when industrialized nations went from wood burning stoves to coal burning, the forests didn't regrow, why? Because so much wood was needed for pit-props, to hold up the coal mine shafts. We were no longer burning it for fuel, but nevertheless the wood demand didn't reduce. And now, with increased population growth, 4 billion people in my youth compared to now, more biomass is burnt than ever.

At present, the entire industrialized world runs on fossil fuels. Do you have a car, a furnace for winter heat? Do you eat? If it's not organic, most food is grown with fossil fuel fertilizer, sprayed with pesticides and herbicides made from fossil fuels. Our food is harvested using massive fossil fuel vehicles, and transported thousands of miles using more fossil fuel vehicles. Yes, we have to phase out fossil fuels to stop burning up the planet. But the whole human-made world would collapse if we did it overnight. One barrel of oil delivers 5-years-work of an adult human! However, it's going to literally run out at some point in the not-too-distant future, so I'd like to suggest we continue to reduce its use as much as possible, to push that run-out date as far off as possible, so that our grandchildren will have its benefit and a longer timeline to make the switch to more sustainable energy supplies – if that's even possible with the consumption demand of 8 billion plus people.

OK - on to the Future Sustainable Neighborhood. My neighborhood is in South-East Pennsylvania, USA, also known as the Delaware Valley or Mid-Atlantic region; 40th parallel north, same as Sardinia. Current temperatures range from approximately 5 degrees F (-15 C) in winter, to 95 degrees F (35 C) in summer.

PART 1: THE WHATS?
HOUSEHOLD ENERGY: OVERVIEW OF SYSTEMS: Centralized energy sources

Currently, most of us in the industrialized countries get our household energy from centralized sources that include: electricity generated by nuclear, natural gas, coal, and in some areas, wind, commercial solar and hydro.

Electricity is fairly easy to distribute through cable systems, even to remote buildings, but other sources of energy are not. For instance, natural gas is supplied directly by extensive underground pipe infrastructure for home heat furnaces and water heaters, mainly in dense population areas; but extensive pipe infrastructure is not economic for sparse rural populations. Consequently, these areas receive their home heating fuels for furnace and water heater use in the form of oil or liquified propane gas, stored in tanks and delivered by trucks.

A heat pump is an electric furnace that simply put, has two car-like radiators, one inside the furnace and one outside the building. Freon is pumped between these and as it compresses or expands, it releases or removes heat. Also, in this furnace, is a large fan that forces air over and through the internal radiator and then around the house in a closed loop system, with no outside air contact. Hence the generic term "forced air system."

Another forced air system, the most common at present, is heated by gas. In this case gas burns inside a metal chamber, heating it, while the large fan blows air over the outside of the chamber, not in contact with the flames – then, around the house. Forced air systems have large air filters that the homeowner should replace, or in some cases, clean from time to time.

Oil and gas can also be used to heat water and make steam, which travels through pipes to room radiators. These used to be the most common types of furnaces, the radiators slowly releasing their heat, whereas forced air systems just heat the air and tend to run more often to keep up. However, to have central air conditioning you need a forced air system.

There are also home-sized geothermal furnaces. They need electricity to run, and are also heat pumps that extract heat from water flowing through shallow buried pipes and other variations of this, heated by the warmth just below ground, (See: BELOW FROSTLINE PHENOMENON). They are also more expensive to install. It's good to know what kind of system you have so when a problem arises you can let contractors know before they arrive.

Is any of this sustainable? Only electricity generated by wind turbines, commercial and home solar and hydro turbines, meets this definition. All the various forms of fossil fuels can sustain for some time longer, until they run out, and there are dates for that, because these stocks are ultimately finite and not renewable.

Staying with the centralized supply, here are a couple of emergency fixes. I have a small non-vented natural gas wall heater that works during electricity outages. One winter, this heated a floor of my house because my old-style heat pump couldn't keep up with

with the extreme cold. Gas pressure is usually maintained in pipes even during power outages, but most gas/oil furnaces also need a small amount of electricity to function – energize the thermostat, run a fan, oil or water pump. If you modify the cable coming into the furnace with a plug and outlet, you can use a small generator to keep the heat on and it's a safe way to isolate the generator from the house wire circuitry. A portable power station/unit can also be used in the same way, just for the furnace. Of course, if you can afford it, a professionally installed whole-house generator, preferably powered by your natural or propane gas supply, ready to go when there's a power cut, is the current ideal for emergency. Fortunately, in the small 13,000 resident rural town where I live, power cuts are rare. The large customer base probably favors us over the surrounding rural areas. But I did just increase my vulnerability to power cuts by switching out my 25-year-old natural gas stove for an electric. But I'm so glad I did, my congestion level last winter was so much reduced, and I think because I had open flame ignition on the old stove. So, I'm going to put a small camping stove in the cupboard for emergencies.

Non-vented gas wall heater

Power backups come in various sizes, this one sufficient to run a gas steam boiler. Put a plug and outlet on main wire in and unplug and plug into unit in an emergency.

Renewable energy is the people's power:
What can individuals do to raise the sustainability and self-reliance of their home/transport energy needs? Let's look at our options.

Solar energy:
Two kinds. Personal solar photovoltaic panels that generate electricity. Solar hydronic panels, that do not produce electricity, but contain fluids in their pipes that absorb heat from the sun, then you can pump this hot fluid to somewhere else for some use.

First, solar photovoltaic panels.
The way we use solar photovoltaic panels has changed over the years. But let's consider what we do now. Today, most panel installations generate electricity that is fed straight to the main electric grid, using an inverter that is part of the system. Then, the building takes its daily electricity from the grid, so it doesn't matter if it's a cloudy day, the grid supply is consistent. The feed-in tariff of the building owner's solar electric supply should pay for itself. However, if the grid goes down, the home also loses power, unless your system has another inverter to send the electricity from your panels directly to your building, which is now common.

Of course, if the grid stays down, night times will need a generator just like everyone else. Hopefully, large home-sized batteries will be available soon to store the daytime solar energy for night time use. Also, some people are using Lithium Iron Phosphate batteries (LFP) wired together, that can be charged by solar generated electricity or direct from the grid.

Consider this: put 150% of your electricity needs in generating power on your roof or property, run a heat-pump furnace, a heat-pump or electric domestic water heater and an electric cooking stove (they are so much better now than the old versions). But, wait, also run an electric vehicle, which charges off your panels. Sounds like that's covered all home energy needs and transport for at least 20 years! Chances are there are large savings here, even if one has to finance it. Is it time to electrify everything? And how about the reduction in carbon footprint?

The brains of a solar system

Heat pumps find it hard to keep up during very cold nights. So, they're usually fitted with an electric or gas backup inside the machine for what's referred to as "emergency heat." If you're not supplying electricity from your own solar panels, this can get expensive.

Another way to store electricity during the day, for night time use, is with electric thermal storage heaters. I grew up in a house with these as our sole heat source, and I realized we can use them for solar systems. They are cabinets, the size of a room radiator, containing fire bricks, with a metal coil intertwined on each layer.

The coil heats up for a portion of the day, storing heat in the bricks, then the bricks release their heat throughout the night. This would work great for winter emergencies when the grid is down. It's also a form of what's called a thermal battery. These can be designed at any scale, even for industrial use and I dare say they will be part of the solar-power future.

Example:
Electric Thermal Storage Unit
https://www.steffes.com

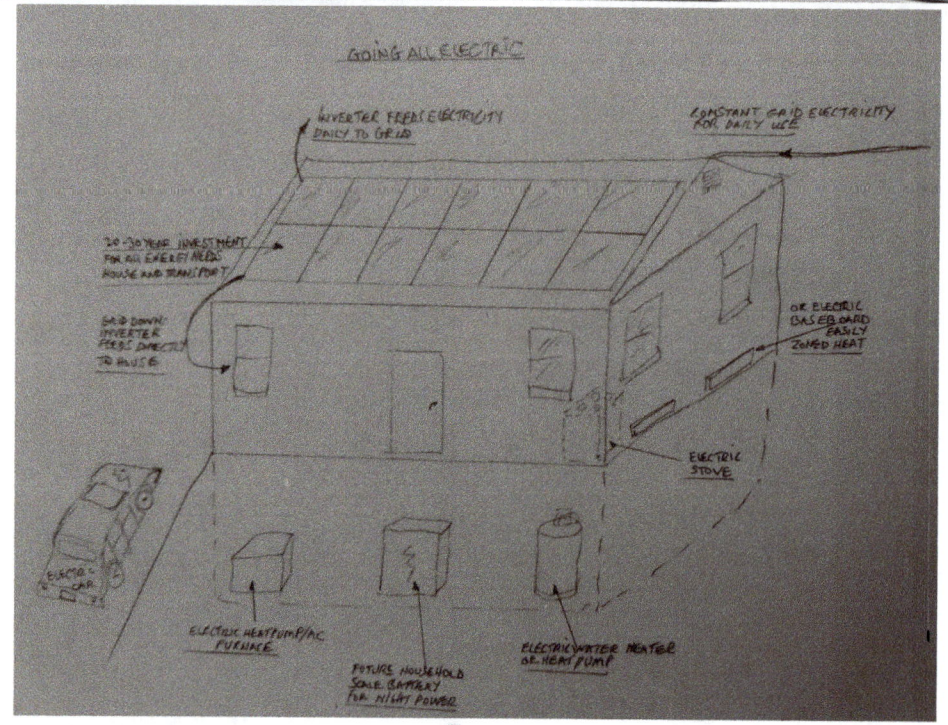

Solar hydronic panels

These produce heat only. In climates like the Middle East and the surrounding area, they're very successful at heating domestic hot water. They could also work for greenhouse space or soil heat. They may be adopted more in the future if energy becomes more expensive and/or less available.

I made a version of hydronic panels for space heat. I constructed and placed a 10 feet x 12 feet panel with copper pipes and aluminum sheets on my roof to heat a 250-gallon (1,000 liter) water tank in line with my forced air system. It pre-warmed the air somewhat for about 10 years before wearing out. If I hadn't used my own labor to make and install it, I don't think it would have been financially viable. I should have spent the money on negawatts first: insulation. (Note: Insolation is the amount of solar energy reaching a surface.)

Home-sized wind turbine

I don't know if there will ever be home-sized wind turbines with sufficient useful power. Some might claim there already are. However, once you've got the solar infrastructure to carry the current into the grid and/or direct to your house; for night-time use it may facilitate a wind turbine. The costs still appear prohibitive and, number one, you've got to have the perfect location with guaranteed continuous wind velocity, which may be good for wind generation, but not an ideal place to situate a house!

Community energy solutions

There are many examples of community solar panel installations around the world. Formed much like coops, where each member is a shareholder. Neighborhood or community scale battery storage on every corner as envisaged in the FSN would be ideal, but as yet, that is a future scenario.

In the future, we may see industrial geothermal plants that can tap the heat from thousands of feet down, to drive neighborhood scale steam turbines. The current skilled employees of the fossil fuel industry would be the perfect workforce to tackle this, as oil and gas extraction wanes.

Personal woodstove energy

Wood burning, a thing of the past? No, more people burn wood now world-wide than any time in history, why? Cause there's more people. Carbon neutral? – kind of, (it's complicated). Great for space heat and cooking. I have a small wood stove in my basement boxed up with everything I need to hook it up, an extreme situation strategy for $150. Wood stoves, for heat and cooking, once the norm, we can do and once established, not dependent on some corporation miles away. We can grow wood on our properties, in our own neighborhoods, with local supply chains. In summer, many do this in the form of barbecue setups, buying charcoal, but we can make our own in a push.

BELOW FROSTLINE PHENOMENON:
Passive space cooling, heating and food storage

And, it's getting hotter all the time. In the FSN we need to survive the cold of winter and the hot of summer. So, in the future, houses with basements/cellars are going to be premium. Why? because you can escape to the basement winter or summer. Friends shared with me, that back in the 1960s their grandparents would serve dinner in the basement during the hot summer weeks, with a rug, table and chairs already set out. On worst days, they'd put a bowl of ice nearby and use an electric fan to blow the air over the ice toward themselves. It's an amazing thing that below the frost line, the soil is about 45 - 50 degrees F (7-9C) all over the world, winter or summer. The frost line refers to the depth to which the ground freezes below the surface in winter (36 inches [90cm] in my town). If we know about this phenomenon and others, we can use them to our advantage.

This is not dependent on above ground temperature, but comes from below. We have proof of its utility. Below is a root cellar in my town built in 1850, well before electric refrigeration.

Root cellar (1850)
- 36" below ground, constant
- temperature 45-50 degrees F

This phenomenon has multiple uses in any country, and could play a part in an ever warming world.

To prevent stored food from freezing in winter: carrots, cabbages, potatoes, winter squash, apples, onions, parsnips, celery, pears, herbs, sweet potatoes, beans, nuts,

Relative postion to kitchen door

Before winter, people filled these cellars with long-lasting produce like cabbage, collards, greens, etc., root crops: carrots, potatoes, parsnips, turnips; onions, apples, leeks, winter squash, etc. And the reason in my neighborhood wasn't to keep the produce super cold, but to keep it between 45–50 (7-9C) degrees so it didn't freeze during the frigid winters. Most basements won't serve this purpose because they are often too warm, unless you understand all this and section off an area with insulation to isolate from the heat and cold, taking advantage of the below frostline surfaces. This may have been learned from the Native people, because a lot of Europeans, especially the English and Irish, were coming from fairly mild countries, and wouldn't have been aware of this useful phenomenon, until they experienced the extreme seasonal temperatures swings in the "new" world.

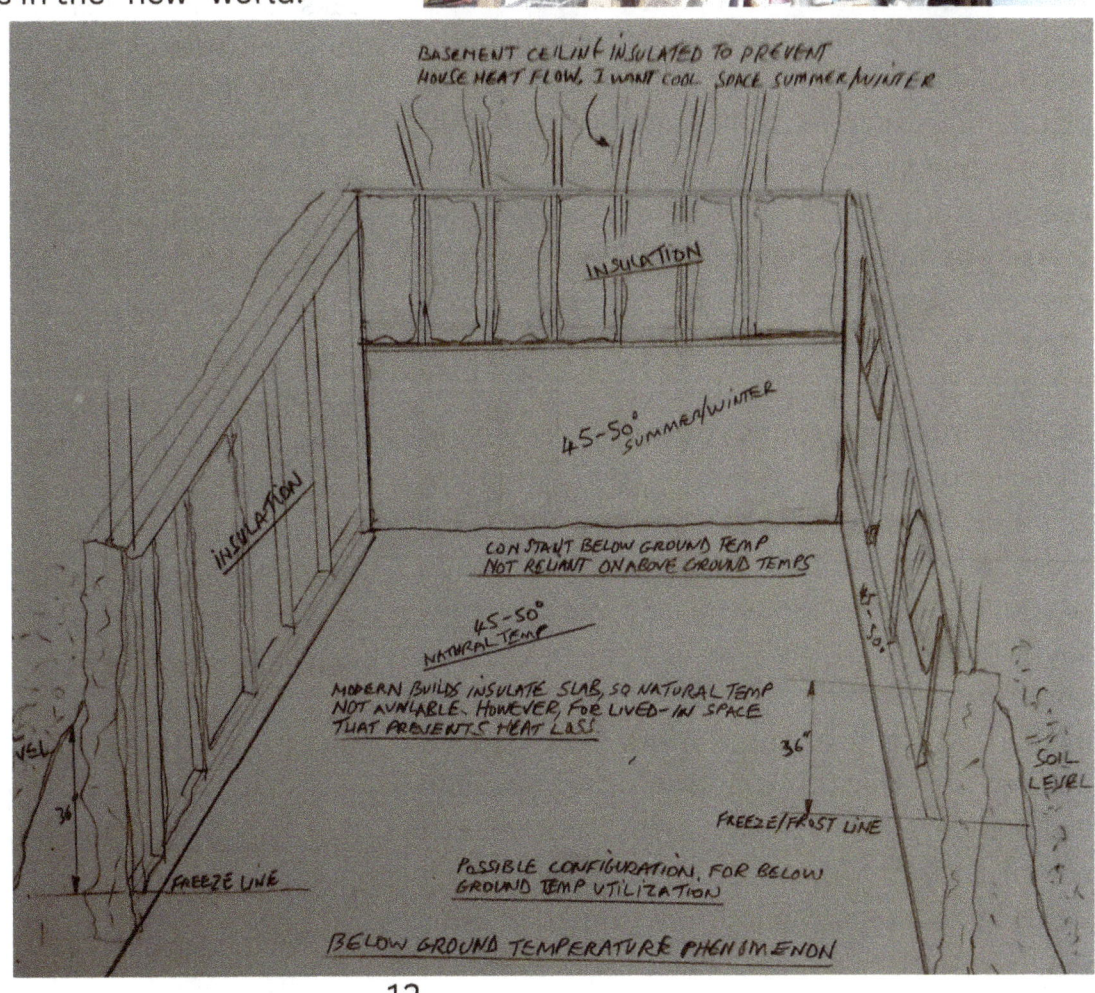

In winter, the floor of the basement has this constant temperature, and in a push, during a prolonged power outage, could remain well above freezing and be livable with cots and sleeping bags, especially if there was a small non-electric heater available.

See the detailed drawing of basement – There may be circumstances where someone would want to customize their basement, keeping these below ground temperature surfaces in mind, for storage and extreme weather living space.

At minimum, you can also sink a metal garbage can in the ground, with the top below the frost line, and use that to store food, then place straw or some kind of insulated material on top of the can.

In rural areas those with larger properties may also have spring-houses built over a natural spring where ground water emerges. The small shed-like buildings protect the water quality from animal influence. Large slabs of slate were partially submerged in the water, dairy products like cheese and milk were placed there using the cooler temperature to preserve them in summer. These phenomena helped people in the past, and we may need them in the FSN, or use them to inspire 'natural' innovations. Because of chemical and industrial pollution soaking into the ground, from the properties that surround them, this shallow groundwater isn't safe to drink nowadays.

Most of the world wastes 40% of food produced! In the industrialized nations they say it happens at the household level, but in countries with less industrialized infrastructure, it happens more from field to market. So, I was thinking, in Africa they could build underground store houses (root cellars) where they could store produce from their fields as it awaits the journey to market. This could also benefit local villages as long as they could prevent animal intrusion, maybe with old shipping containers?

NEGA-WATTS

No watts used, not kilowatts (thousand watts) or megawatts (million watts), that means INSULATE. No matter what your resources are or what system you have, this is a benefit to all.

We need government programs or mega-wealthy foundations to subsidize everyone to insulate their buildings to the maximum to reduce energy use, reduce CO_2 impacts and free up energy for other electrification demands. The most effective two things in this area, from what I've seen, is insulating the highest ceiling in the building to R40, about 12 inches (30 cm) of fiberglass insulation, and stopping the air-chimney-effect through the house – from incoming leaks in the basement and ground floor doors, windows, etc., and fixing outgoing leaks all the way up the structure to the roof. Be aware of the need for airflow between the insulation and the roof, to minimize condensation that can rot wood. Instead of subsidizing nuclear power plants, using billions of taxpayer's dollars and long development time, conserve first, then see how much we need. 25 - 50% energy saved nationwide? Centuries of benefit starting now, with huge employment opportunities (Unfortunately, the last thing today's medieval corporations and mega-rich elite want to do is empower citizens, who are only seen as consumers, creatures to be exploited, isolated, disempowered and made dependent. There was a short-lived earlier time when pro-social elite enabled employee pensions and a living wage, but, sadly, that time has now passed!)

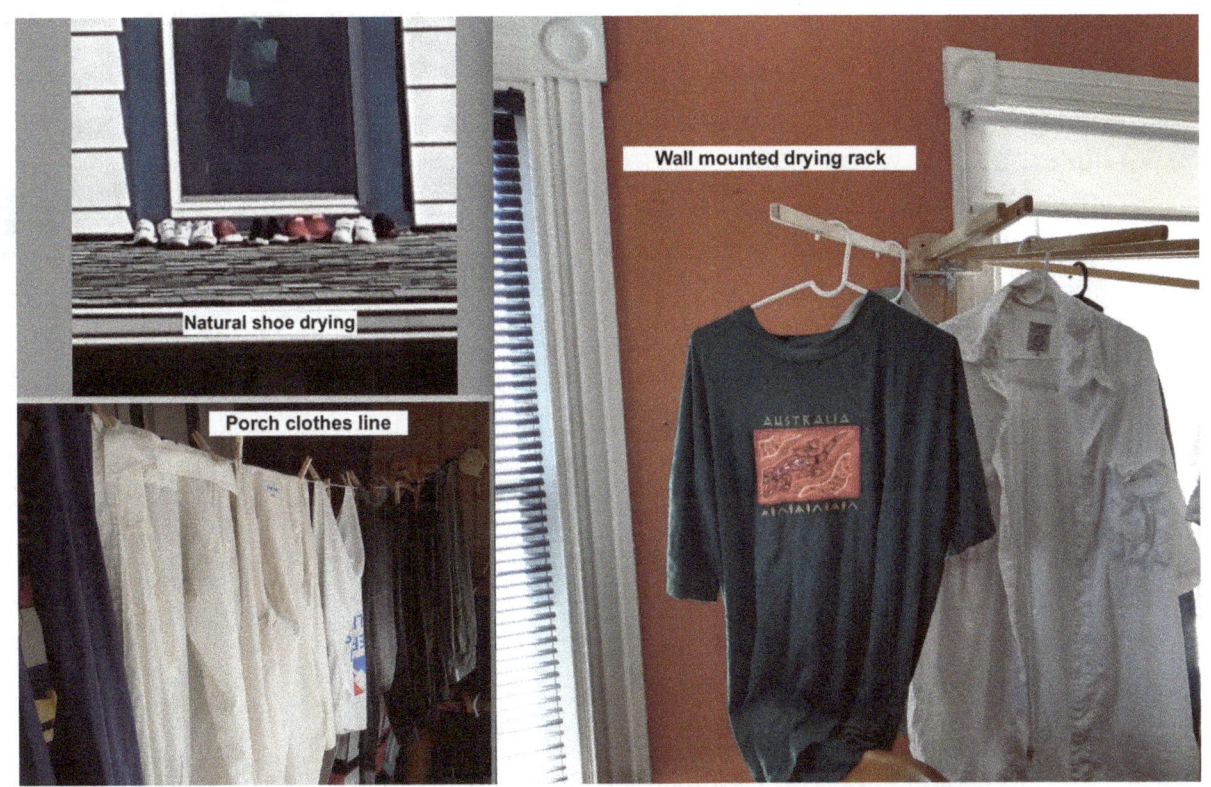

Black aluminum blinds to capture winter heat gain

NO NUCLEAR:

Jane Jacobs, in her book, Cities and the Wealth of Nations, speaks of "transactions of decline." These happen when countries fail to understand the real reasons for their economic decline, so they introduce measures like: 'unremitting-subsidies' and false solutions, which slow decline, but eventually make the decline more catastrophic. I see reverting to nuclear power generation as lack of imagination that could stifle innovation. All we are doing, after all, is boiling water to run turbines. Can't we do better than this 30-year lifespan, thousands of years baby-sitting old infrastructure, huge expense storing used radio-active waste, and huge taxpayer subsidies for industry? Insulate instead. Surely, placing this on future generations is a moral failure, and should it fail, now or later, would devastate nature itself. Will future generations even be able to take care of all the world-wide obsolete atomic power structures, for thousands of years, to prevent radiation leaks, without the advantage of fossil fuels?

EXTERIOR COOL/HEAT STRATEGY

Continuing with heat reduction, in the FSN we will paint all of our flat roofs with light colored paints or aluminum roof coatings, if they're still available, to reduce the heat in the space between the roof and ceiling, which in turn reduces heat gain on the upper floors. Of course, solar panels also help the roof stay cooler, from the shading created by the air gap between panels and roof. This air gap could be replicated on any roof by placing an extra lightweight covering over a building.

Also, I used a dark color on my south-facing exterior wall to warm my house in winter – which leads to:

SUMMER/WINTER SUN ANGLE PHENOMENON:

Another natural phenomenon we need to know about is the sun's path, winter and summer and why it's important and how we can use it to our advantage. Did you know there are two easts and two wests? Take a look at the illustration. It's hard to believe in the height of summer that the sun will drop so low in the sky during winter, but it does, as seen here (23 degrees). This allows the sun's rays to penetrate under the roof into the space and some way up the wall. We can use this. In summer the sun's path goes almost vertically over the building, starting a little north of east and setting a little north of west. At these times the sun actually shines briefly on the north side of my house. This all leads to:

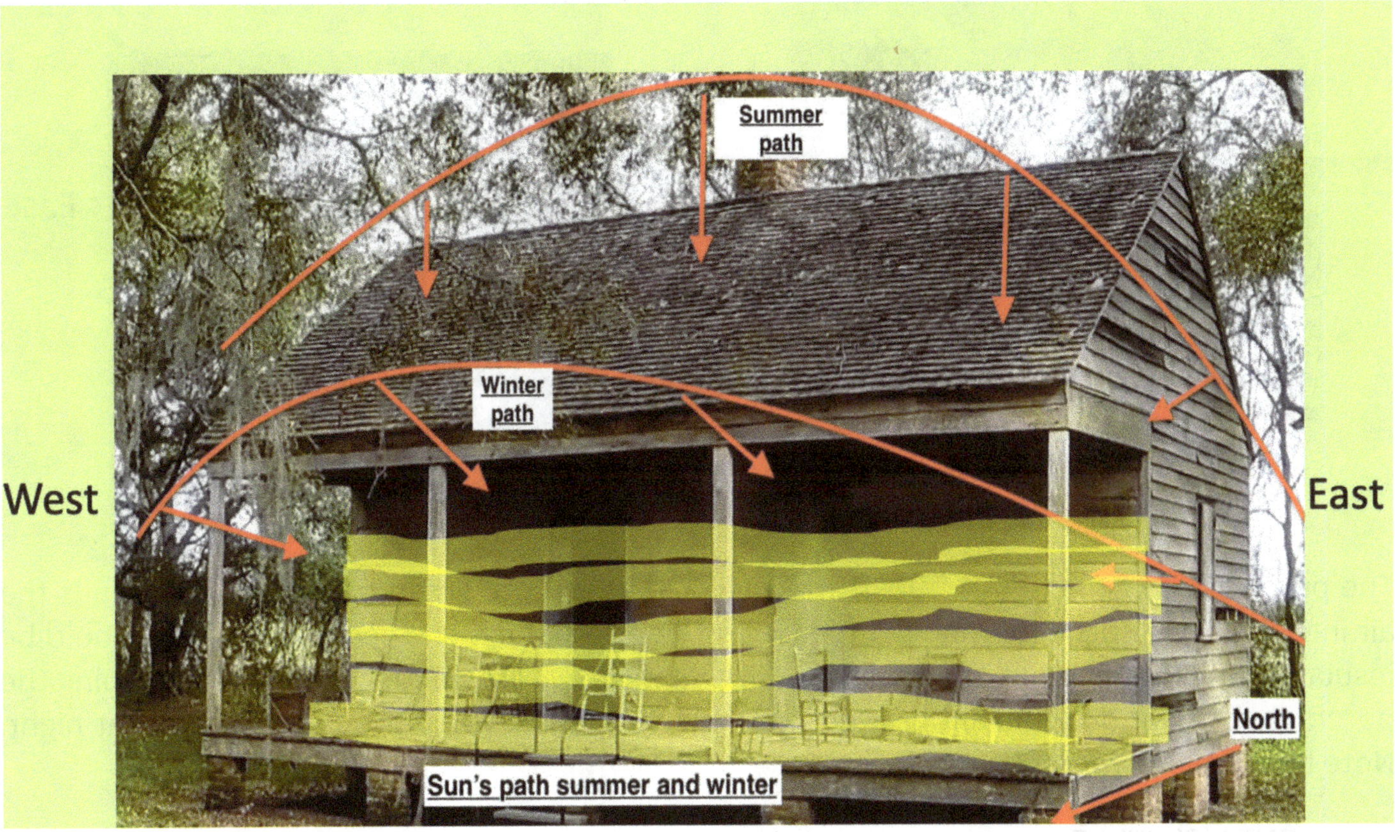

Sun-penetrable structures

Glass and polycarbonate covered structures connected to southern exposure of buildings, great for passive heat in winter, extended edible plant growing and all-winter growing.

It's too hot in my region for just glass, but for shade, grow vines that leaf out in summer, or use shade cloth. Adds value and interesting space to any house, helps with winter growing and season extension.

East
South

The porch above goes to 80º - 90ºF in winter and a fan connected to a thermostat pulls the air into the living space for much of the day for home heating. The ceiling and floor should be insulated when it becomes an interior porch and windows are opened in summer, keeping the porch cool. I heat only the air, not the thermal mass, because I don't use the space at night. Note blue wall for winter heat gain.

RESILIENT LIFESTYLE
An ongoing list of suggestions to act on now – to be better positioned as we enter the Sustain-Age.

Reduce expenses across the board:
No frivolous buying, this is at the heart of economic self-preservation
Save energy by draft-proofing your house or business, this goes before insulation
Zone the house or apartment in winter by turning off heat in rooms with no water and close doors, or hang curtains to prevent unnecessary heating and cooling. Don't forget, cold air falls like water, so close off 2nd floor to prevent coolness falling to lower levels.
Install a simple set-back thermostat that can turn down heat when you're away, unless you have a heat-pump, because they don't recover well from temperature drops. I turn down the temperature on my hot water tank from May to November, when the incoming water is a little warmer anyway; also, always use cold rather than heated water when you can. Conserve energy everywhere: work, home, driving style.

Transport:
Seek transport for best return on fuel investment.
Try to work as close to home as possible.
Figure out the real costs of commuting over an hour each way – time, gas, wear and tear on car, stress, because taking a lower wage may be possible if you live nearer to work.
Move near to public transport.
Plan trips in your car, don't just run out for every little thing, group trips together, plan. Our world has been designed by the car and the fossil-fuel industry, not wisdom, sustainability or livability. It's time to redesign for all life in the biosphere. What if we designed our workplace to be reachable by bicycle? It used to be, but the car allowed us to live so far from the workplace, and now we waste so much valuable time commuting. Progress? You decide!

Join community:
We all live in a community, but not all communities communicate. That means, we have to talk to people, maybe someone has a solution, an innovation; communication leads to opportunity, sharing, peace of mind, support...etc.

Work:
What will the Sustain-Age need?
Many jobs haven't even been conceived of yet.
People gardening/growing food increases every year (how much do you spend on food that you could grow?)
We may need to have multiple streams of income from small-scale initiatives. E.g., carpenter fixes house and makes objects for sale at markets, also teaches others to reskill.
There may be a large swing to relocalization. Look for opportunities, form networks.
Consider what you can do at the household economy level. (See: The Household Economy.)
Don't be a one-trick pony - the more skills we have the better equipped we'll be. We're not very practical now in a post-industrial world. We need PDFs but we can't just be a PDFer! These extra skills are not necessarily corporately marketable, but at least useful to the Sustain-Age.
The janitor and the lawyer must become amateur ecologists.

Home:
Have at least one month of food in the house for everyone, canned foods that don't need cooking, just warming, dried goods like rice, beans and grains, packaged pasta, drinking water (1/2 gallon a day each person), etc.
Use a bread machine for bread (80cents a loaf (with machine costs) instead of as much as $5 and you control the salt, etc., in it. Or use salt, water, flour and yeast and knead it yourself (I do now, having worn out many bread machines,) bake three loaves at a time and put two in the freezer.
Cook more of your own food for better health. Anything you buy from a corporation is made from the cheapest edible substances, sugar only adds weight, to maximize profits, not your nutrition and health.
Plan cooking. Maybe Sunday afternoon cook for a few days' supply and store in fridge.
Don't forget a vacuum flask can keep soups, hot water, pre-made drinks hot or cold all day.
If you have even a small piece of yard surface that gets sun for minimum of 6 hours a day, plant something to give you a harvest, it's very easy. At least build soil now for when you'll need it and/or be directly in touch with those who grow your food.
According to ratings, most people still watch an average of 4 hours of TV or social media a day. That's a quarter of our awake day, every day. That's equivalent to 3.5 x 8hour work days a week – lots of time to educate and prepare ourselves (the great thing is you can cook and watch TV!)
Our hot water tanks, often in our basements, contains 40 – 80 gallons. If there is an emergency it can be accessed from the silt-drainage spout at its base. Let it run to clear the silt, this is not the best water to drink, but for everything else. In fact, open the silt drain every year or so to clean it out.

Time Bank:
Many "Time-Banks" with over a hundred members, gives us a great non-cash resource to barter our corporate and minor skills. And because there are so many people in the "Bank," we can trade our time for so many

other different skills, not just the person who served us. This frees up our cash for the money economy. More info: http://timebanks.org/

Visioning:
Overcome the fear of many modern people for taking on physical activities like gardening, cooking, repairing; although it was everyone's wish to get 'off the farm,' today, with our new insights, activities don't have to be grueling.

Look to sustainable and Transition initiatives (Transitionnetwork.org), to get a jump on what the Sustain-Age might look like now and in 3, 5, 7, 10, 15 years. What are people who are thinking about this stuff saying? More info: Modern lifestyles, actions and business will need to be guided by Permaculture principles and the ethics of Earth care, People care and Fair share to prevent further damage to the ecosystem and injustices: wholistic thinking approach. (See: SYSTEMS THINING.)

Place based awareness:
Where is the fire, flood, landslide, sink-holes, toxic air coming from in your neighborhood? Can you mitigate/prepare for their arrival ahead of time? Fire often comes from the direction of the prevailing wind, which in my neighborhood is from the west (westerlies). Up-wind of your property, are there any kinds of: automobile businesses (spray paint), scrap yards, industrial complexes, that if malfunctioned could cause you risk? We have a small river moving through town, but it is so deep in its location that it is not a flood risk. However, free-wheel on my bicycle and it will show you where the unofficial flood areas are – low spots trapped by other streets. If the street drains weren't blocked underground this wouldn't be a problem, but they are blocked, so streets full of rain end up flooding these low spots. The modern world's infrastructure was built over a hundred-year period, now we can't afford the trillions of dollars it takes to maintain it! Your parallel, north or south of the equator, informs you of how many hours of sunlight are available per day. Also, your average temperatures, first and last frost dates. Can you glean any useful history about your location from your neighbors? Don't just live in your head or electronic devices; get to truly know and nurture your earthly location, it enriches our life.

Know energy:
Know your energy use:
What is your 'base load' energy need? The 'base load' is your monthly use, in say, May or late September in the northern hemisphere, when you need the least help from mechanical systems to heat or cool your house. In other words: furnace, heaters, and air conditioners are turned off. So, it's just lights, cooking stove, electrical appliances, domestic hot water that you're paying for. (Windows open all day are a sign of a 'base load' month.) My base load is $75.00 a month. If I have guests or family members staying with me it increases per person.

We should all know our base load because then we'll understand how much extra energy we use for cooling in summer (summer load) and heating in winter (winter load).

All this can be gleaned from your energy bill. And don't forget that most bills reflect the use of the previous month. Just be clear about which month you're looking at. You'll want to familiarize yourself with this bill because it will be your gauge to see if you've managed to increase your negawatts, the ones you don't use. Also, if you are comparing different months or years, look at the average temperature for the month, it is on the bill, because even one degree rise or fall affects your energy demand and you can't make accurate comparisons without that.

258 kWh   X   0.06100   15.74

COST → $45.0

Your Usage Profile

USAGE

Period	Usage	Avg Daily Usage	Days	Avg Daily Temp
Current Month	258	8.6	30	68
Last Month	219	7.5	29	58
Last Year	229	7.6	30	69
Avg kWh per Month				295
Total Annual kWh Usage				3,545

YEAR COMPARISON

More actions:
Check chimneys for closed dampers, otherwise there is a hole to the sky!
Place and caulk insulation panel in unused chimney.
Install a programmable thermostat.
Put automatic damper on furnace exhaust.
Install low-flow faucets and showerhead.
Replace all lighting with LEDs.
Clean (vacuum) dryer vents or replace and make sure flap closes on outside.
Vacuum refrigerator coils every 3 years, it will last longer and be more efficient.
Bleed air from room radiators when heat is on.
Humidify in winter to feel warmer and prevent dried throat.
At beginning of winter, if you have them, check lower storm windows are down and higher ones are pushed all the way up.
Caulk storm windows at window frame, to reduce drafts.

When replacing appliances:
Don't buy higher efficiency appliances, to save money, until current unit is worn out. Then replace with high efficiency products, or if you've installed solar panels, go all electric and consider tankless water heaters. Move water heater closer to main faucet when replacing, or immediately if you have an electric heater.

Energy Resilience Assessments:
Businesses and citizens need to do Energy Resilience Assessments to figure out how to react to an energy stressed future and where you might want to trigger alarms. For instance, does $5 a gallon gasoline mean you can't afford to take the car to work anymore? Do you have a public transport alternative? Did you vote against that spending for public transport at the last election?
At what point does your home energy costs jeopardize your ability to pay the mortgage? Then, when is the time to start powering down and implementing these ideas?

Renovating or re-modeling:

Are you thinking of renovating or re-modeling? That is an ideal time to become more sustainable. If you're going to build a new structure, consider 8 -12 inch external walls, 30-40 R value, single two by four inch lumber is not Sustain-Age thinking. If you're renovating and could lose a few inches in the room, consider adding insulating panel to the interior walls. Orientate your new structure to the south and take advantage of solar gain. Consider the quality, size and design of things like windows, doors and lighting. In short, design your new space to serve you and sustainability.

12 inch (30cm) walls:

Two 2" (5 cm) x 4" (10 cm) stud frames separated by a 2" x 12" top plate as in the picture, filled with R19 insulation from both sides will give about an R40 wall. With an R40 ceiling, heating and cooling energy needs for the enclosed space will be minimal. Extra work and money up front, you ask, of course? But then negligible energy bills forever, it's worth it. You can reduce to a 2" x 8" wall if using a sprayed expanding foam product to give the same advantage and an even more air-tight wall.

Insulated panel:

If you're renovating and can't open up the walls, but can bare to lose a few inches in the room, consider adding insulated panel to the inside of exterior walls with sheet rock (dry wall) glued to them. You gain R5 insulation values for each inch (1.5 cm) of paneling added. On many older stone-walled homes in Pennsylvania, there is little or no insulation between the plaster wall and the exterior wall. This is a way to add insulation, but of course moldings, etc., have to be removed, so only if you're renovating anyway.

A one-inch sheet can also be used inside closets where mold may form due to the coldness of the exterior facing wall, especially in old stone wall construction. Because the closet door is closed, it is colder inside and condensation forms on the wall to feed the mold. I screw this straight to the plastered/stone surface with 2 or 2 ½ inch hardened, self-driving screws, they'll grab the plaster, don't over-screw them, and put some adhesive on the high spots of the wall, then caulk or plaster to seal air from getting to the old wall. It works like a charm. For new construction there are SIPs (Structurally Insulated Panels) that can be used.

Take control:

The bottom line is, in the Sustain-Age, we have to be engaged citizens. Our decisions cannot be passive, but informed by our sustainable awareness, because even the contractor you employ for a renovation, may not be sustain-aware yet. This may mean that you have to explain your principles of design. This will usually be decided at the architect stage. Even if the walls are fantastically insulated, it won't matter if doors and windows leak. So, the whole package must be considered.

A renovation is a good time to consider a 'safe room' in your house. Which room needs the least energy to keep warm if there were an energy crisis during the winter? A new renovation, using some of the ideas above, could become that space. Preferably with least windows, in case of tornadic winds. Ideally well insulated. A basement will suffice, but not during floods. A living room with a wood stove, or a place for a kerosene heater for single-room heat, etc. Cool rooms are lower in the building during summer. Utilizing natural cooling, ground floor apartments on the north side of buildings, will be most coveted in future.

ORGANIC EDIBLE GARDENING LIFESTYLE:

There's a lot to learn, but by the end of this section you'll know more than enough to get you started, or, if you're already a gardener, you will pick up a useful tidbit.

We use gasoline, diesel or electric to fuel our transport. We use plant and animal matter, to fuel our body engines – our stomachs. So why not grow our own fuel/energy!?

The U.S. produces all the calories it needs. However, approximately 50% of fruits and vegetables come from Mexico, so this is misleading. I was looking around the data about other countries' ability to be self-sufficient in food, most are not, but some it said were, and then there are the anomalies like the U.S. example above. Most countries rely on stable international trade and shipping to feed themselves.

Did you notice any food shortages during the Pandemic of the early 2020s? The fact is, no one is running the worldwide food system, it's a market wonder of demand and supply. According to the Delaware Valley Regional Planning Commission, we grow 6% of our food in the Philadelphia region where I live, does that sound like food security to anyone?

Most food in the U.S. travels minimum 1,500 miles to market. At my locally owned and operated whole foods health store, where I shop almost exclusively, there were almost no shortages during the Pandemic – why? Because the owner has a philosophy of sourcing from dozens of local farms and suppliers.

Some good news, about two in five American households now practice some food growing in their gardens, approximately 50 plus million homes. And whenever there is a crisis, for example, a pandemic, those numbers increase. That warms my heart, it means we're not all sleep-walking.

It seems to me, that never before industrial modernism has an entire population outsourced its food supply to far-off shores, over which it has little control. I was thinking, well, Tony, that hasn't been a problem in your lifetime, why alert people to this now? And that's true, however, most people have outsourced their food supply to industry, not farms. Three hospitals have closed in the last 2 years within 30 miles of my home. Corporate profit-based interests running and wrecking the health system from within, run by accountants, not healthcare professionals. Add to that, the public eating and behaving irresponsibly, expecting the healthcare system to bail them out. Many people in my town overconsume processed foods (engineered to be addictive), that don't supply sufficient human nutrition, leading to some of my neighbors dying in their early sixties. So, although there have not been "edible substance" shortages, there are serious detrimental effects from the current food system, with multiple health problems occurring for years before the onset of death. "In the U.S. we have a diet related disease epidemic," Dariush Mozaffarian, Director, Food is Medicine Institute, Tufts University. TAKE CONTROL! Read, Food Fix, by Mark Hyman, MD.

So, let's get with this:
Earlier, garden designs brought the farm into the garden with lots of rows and space between them for machinery, but we don't need to do that now. Raised beds are now popular, and can even be placed in the middle of a lawn or asphalt surface; and the grass can't get to them, nor the grass cutter! Soil compaction is eliminated, that means, you're in no doubt of where the growing area is and you shouldn't step on it. Beds shouldn't make you stretch more than 2 feet (60cm), otherwise you'll be tempted to step in them. By preventing this, you'll have softer soil for roots, water and air to spread, this leads to higher yields of food. (see: SOME GARDENING LIFESTYLES).

And, by the way, if you plant a fruit tree, don't be in a hurry. Dig a wide hole with lots of great, loose soil in it and the roots of the tree will take off, establish quicker and give you fruit sooner. And no mulch volcanoes up the trunk, and don't plant the flare, where the tree was grafted onto sturdy stock, below the surface level, (see: TREES IN THE FSN).

If you set up the beds correctly, you'll be almost weed free. What? Yep! Even if you see weeds always get them out of the bed before they flower and go to seed; because then, each year, you'll reduce weed pressure. And the more crowded your plants, the less light gets between them to wake up any weed seeds that might be laying around. Contained beds also reduce soil erosion and make it easy to put a small fence around if you need to.

The main path through the growing area should be about 2 feet wide to accommodate maybe a wheelbarrow. But between beds, 1 foot is fine, because then you're maximizing the growing area. You can use any material to form the beds, but nothing toxic like pressure treated wood or railroad ties. Even if you use these, cover the growing side with a thin layer of something to prevent leaching. Beds don't need to be more than 8 inches (18cm) deep, unless you're planting root vegetables. They need a minimum 6 – 8 hours of sun a day, and the more they get the bigger yield you'll have, (see: SUMMER/WINTER SUN ANGLE-PHENOMENON-and https://squarefootgardening.org). If you're a beginner at edible gardening, buy seedlings – small plants, rather than seeds, for better success.

Pre-drill ends and screw together with 3" screws

Shake plant out of pot supported with fingers and plant in hole

Cut grass inside frame and lay down sheet mulch

Season's end...Ah!!!

Water access is a plus, near enough to a downspout or rainwater container, with whatever system you use to accomplish watering: gravity-fed hose, watering can, drip irrigation, small pond pump with hose, (see: RAINWATER HARVESTING).

Try to avoid high wind and wet areas, and position as near to the house as possible, where you're more likely to go out and collect the harvest. Imagine your property in zones: zone 1, near the kitchen door, herbs and vegetables need to be in this zone so it's easy to harvest them. Zone 2, a little further out, maybe root plants like potatoes and carrots, zone 3 berry bushes and fruit trees, zone 4, semi-wild, not manicured. Of course, an urban property like mine only has one large zone really, but I let stuff go wild around the side of the house for insect populations and the critters passing through day and night. Interplant compatible crops to reduce pest and disease problems. Don't monocrop, put patches of the same plant in different places. Use succession planting for intensive cultivation – when one crop finishes be ready to plant the next one, often a different crop altogether. Use trellises or or cages for vines on north side of beds, if you're in the northern hemisphere, so as not to shade out other produce. Use cold frames and row covers to extend growing season and prevent pests in some cases. Cover plants like leafy vegetables with light-weight row covers for those that don't need pollinators, preventing moths and butterflies depositing their caterpillars – the sun will get through. Reduce weeds using mulches. I like straw, which is the left-over stalks of cereal plants like wheat, but hay is the stalks of grasses, so don't use them for mulch, otherwise left-over seeds will germinate in your garden. You can use wood chips, not black walnut, on the surface, but be careful not to mix it into the soil, otherwise it steals the nitrogen. Of course, there is plastic, but cardboard is great also, if you're not concerned about the look, as it adds carbon to the soil when it breaks down. Once your beds are established there is no need to dig them over each season, become a no-dig gardener, because soil knows best how to structure itself. Each planting season, just dig the size hole you need for the seedling you want to plant, place it in and water for a few days to establish. Likewise with seeds, just shallow rake the soil, sprinkle and water them.

In winter, plant daikon radish that will die back, covering the ground to prevent weeds (cover crop). Let ground covers, like purslane below, grow between plants to shade out weeds while giving you another edible crop. Row covers to protect greens from caterpillars and extend season.

Maintenance:

Once the garden is planted and established, you'll find out it's not just your garden, no other animal recognizes the concept of "my garden," even though they've made no effort to establish it. So, you'll need to protect it and, depending on your location, you'll have different garden visitors. Among the insects about 15% are problematic, 85% working for us. Learn a little about this, utilizing nature's pest management, then you'll be an ecological gardener. Here's a secret, the sooner you remove the first sight of any insect pests or weeds, the less trouble they become and may not even become a problem at all, but if we let them flourish, they can overwhelm us.

Encourage the beneficials. There are 350 species of wild or native bees in my region and they need habitat – holes in wood, holes in the soil, most are soil dwellers, so leave bare patches – most people never notice them but they're doing most of the pollinating. They live alone and are not aggressive, which comes from defending hives. Bumble bees, mason and sweat bees, which we've been killing for decades with pesticides, are doing the work among my plants. The honey bee is a European bee that didn't co-evolve with our ecology but of course people love them for the honey they produce. Their hives can be moved around to facilitate pollination, but they are also threatened by modern agricide practices.

Utilizing nature's pest management

Above: mason bees need holes, they don't make holes like the naughty carpenter bees. The tomato horn work caterpillar has been parasitized by a tiny wasp, so leave them and they will be working for you for years. Also, praying mantis and assassin bugs and bumble bees on sunflower.

Most fruit bushes and trees are perennial. That means plant once, do a little pruning from time to time and harvest for years, we like that. Perennial means that the plant will go dormant in winter and come back to life in the spring. Some plants appear perennial but are not. The plants I'm thinking of are the ones that drop seeds near their last growing position, re-emerging in spring – these are self-seeders, I even have heirloom tomatoes and cucumbers that do this. Uh, oh, that leads to what is heirloom, hybrid, seeds? Heirloom seeds usually have a long history and are open pollinated, meaning the seed from each plant will reproduce every year true to the original. Hybrids are specially crossbred to produce different qualities, often for commercial growers to have sturdier stock, but their seeds don't produce the same variety next year, so don't save them, you might be wasting your time, you have to buy a new supply. GMO types of seeds are primarily used commercially for crops such as corn, soybeans, canola, sugar beets and cotton, so we rarely need to consider those.

Chicken wire styles of cages. Love the ones over my raised beds, reduces squirrel mischief and interference from others. Also low style for winter squash and peanuts.

All sizes, pre-made chicken cages work great for protection. Connect some wooden pieaces to the frame and staple plastic for a winter hoop house. Leave ends covered through summer, just remove center section.

- 1 gallon per 100 square feet (3 x 3 meters)
- 4 parts seed meal (soy)
- 1/3 part lime: dolomite, agricultural
- 1 part rock phosphate
- 1 part kelp

For many years on my property, with the addition of my own compost, I have used exclusively the plant and mineral fertilizer formula above. I buy the ingredients from feed stores in bulk, except for a small bag of rock phosphate from a garden supply and this lasts years for my small property. I got this from Steve Solomon's website: https://soilandhealth.org. The soy-seed-meal supplies the nitrogen and you can also add it to a hugleculture mound if it's too heavy in carbon materials.

Potting soil is quite expensive, and is just soil that has been heated to about 160 F for about 30 minutes to kill any competing seeds that might lurk there, so there's no competition for the seed you are planting.

I do this by putting a layer of soil under glass to heat up in the sun for an hour or so, then mix in a little real compost to lighten it up.

Below: Four layers of newsprint, soaked in salt brine, stapled, dried, cut minimal keyhole to fit around plant - slugs be gone!

Severe weather:

Food growing protection, growing season extension, winter food growing, current and future extreme weather may force us to have systems for covering crops during events. During summer of 2024, for the first time, I put shade cloth over my cages due to severe heat. For a couple of years now, I've thrown a temporary tarp over them during severe downpours.

A mention of **frost vs. freezing** that gardeners need to know. Freezing and frost are not the same. Many plants can freeze and survive but can't survive a frost, it's more of a burning effect. "Frosts can occur even when a thermometer at eye level shows temperatures a few degrees above freezing. On calm, clear nights during the fall, winter, and spring, heat from the ground and within a foot or two of the ground escapes to higher elevations very quickly. Under these conditions, temperatures close to the ground can fall to 32 degrees, while 4 to 5 feet higher the temperature can be several degrees above freezing. In some situations, the 32-degree height may be present for just a few inches above the surface. Water vapor in air right at the surface goes directly from a gas to a solid, creating frost. When temperatures are warmer with height, that's called a temperature inversion. This is a common occurrence on calm, clear nights." (University of Illinois Agriculture Extension.) Sensitive sub-tropical plants like: tomato, egg-plant, green-peppers, etc., can't go into the garden before May 10 in my bio-region because of last frost dates.

Plant Families:

Just like us, plants live in families. Being aware of this allows us to identify plant types, which gives us guidance. For instance, it's best not to put edible plants from the same family in the same garden position every year, because the pests for those plants may winter over in the soil. You can learn a lot more about these families by googling: "Field identification of the 50 most common plant families in temperate regions." For instance, mangoes, cashews and poison ivy are from the same family, that's why eating too many mangoes can unbalance our physiology if we're not used to them. Also, tomatoes, sweet peppers, jalapeno peppers, potatoes, eggplant, are all from the same family! To me it's amazing to learn what is in the same family. In a small garden it is hard to put plants in a different position every year, I've grown potatoes in the same area for ten years. If your soil is in tip-top condition, the plants will be healthy and able to withstand the pests, especially if you're looking out for them.

Weeds?

Develop a foraging mentality, know your edible 'weeds.' The weeds tend to be bitter because they haven't been cultivated for sweetness. However, this can mean that they retain more nutritional value. Here's just a few: dandelion (root, leaf, flower), purple deadnettle and Lamb's quarters. (Identifying and Harvesting Edible and Medicinal Plants, Steve Brill with Evelyn Dean.)

Pollen and Nectar:

The difference between pollen and nectar. Nectar is a little sweet gift a flower gives an insect when it visits. The search for this treat causes the insect to rub its body on the pollen in the flower and then transport it to other flowers, pollinating (fertilizing) them to produce seeds. Most insects can receive nourishment of this sort from multiple different plants, but some, like the monarch butterflies, can only lay their eggs on one plant, in this case milkweed leaves, because the caterpillars can only eat that. No milkweeds, no monarchs next year!

More reasons to grow:

Cut food costs. What do we spend per year @ $10 a day, maybe $3,650 a year for one person? Maybe we could grow 25% of our food needs, and the best part is the fruits and vegetables we grow will be fresher, safer and more nutritious, than store bought. We'll get exercise. It's right outside our back door, less trips to the store. Less traffic time, gas costs, wasting time. Increased food security. Knowledge for life and to share with others. Kids love this, (and being outside), but don't just make them weed slaves, that's a turn-off.

Most gardeners know there's stress relief from being in the garden, touching the soil, feeling the breeze, hearing the birds, being amused by annoying squirrels, etc. Dr. Benjamin Rush 1812:

… "digging in a garden' was one of the activities that distinguished those male patients who recovered from their mania from those that did not." From his book Medical Inquiries and Observations Upon Diseases of the Mind, professor of the Institute of Medicine and Clinical Practice at the University of Pennsylvania, and known for his role in the development of modern psychiatry.

PLANTS DON'T HAVE DOUBT OR ATTITUDE, THEY WANT TO GROW!

Below: daikon radish winter micro-greens, harvest in 10 days

Used coffee-cup lids work great for single serving of daikon radish micro-greens. Put in tray and flood tray to water potting soil, about 10 days later you can harvest - winter food growing.

Herbs:

Growing herbs is an easy way into the organic edible gardening lifestyle. All cultures around the world enjoy them, often from wild plant sources, and we can choose a plethora of plants to grow just outside the kitchen door in zone 1, where we're more likely to go out and grab some. My garden contains: lavender, lemon balm, lemon verbena, sage, oregano, rosemary, and several mint varieties. These can all serve as non-caffeinated 'teas' or for culinary use, and grow fine in containers. There is only one tea plant, camellia sinensis – China, camellia assamica – India, but because the word tea is so associated with hot water poured over plant material, we use 'tea' to also describe herbal beverages, which the French call tisanes. We don't say herbal coffees, do we? To enjoy the various health benefits of the compounds in each one, don't get too stuck on a favorite. You can pick them fresh and pour hot water over, and/or, as I do, dry and store them in airtight containers for months.

If you're currently a big processed food eater, grab some dried herbs, crush them up and sprinkle over that heated pizza or whatever, to give you an extra nutritional benefit. You can learn which herbs traditionally accompany different foods.

Growing herbs not only leads to beverage plants, you'll also be growing home health remedies by default. My short list of anecdotal helpers: Lemon Verbena tea works great for clearing a stuffy head or for lemon flavoring in cooked dishes; Lemon Balm tea is very calming and helps relieve the pain associated with shingles (can be used topically also); Lavender is great for a nightcap tisane; I mix mint with green tea to make it more pleasant, mint is also traditionally used to calm an upset stomach; oregano tea is said to have anti-viral and anti-bacteria properties. There is so much information about this today, (See: James A. Duke, Ph.D., The Green Pharmacy, and the National Geographic Guide to Medicinal Herbs).

My regular cooking herbs, bought and grown, include: Turmeric, paprika, oregano, parsley flakes, cumin, sage, lavender, rosemary, lemon verbena, ginger, mint, basil, coriander powder, black pepper (usually as a condiment). Sparingly: cloves, fenugreek seeds, marjoram, nutmeg, cayenne pepper.

Making my favorite apple-mint tisane, harvested from the garden.

Various methods of drying (dehydrating) herbs. Brown paper bag in car back window is the most awesome! But for "wet" veggies like tomato or purslane, heat and a fan are needed to prevent mould.

Some Gardening Styles:

During your exploration into the FSN you're bound to come across references to different gardening methods, so I've featured a few of the most common ones here.

Conventional gardening, which of course is not conventional at all but modern, uses industrial chemicals from fossil fuels in its production.

Organic gardening pioneered by J. I. Rodale, "Organic farmers rely on natural processes, biodiversity, and cycles adapted to local conditions rather than the use of synthetic inputs like chemical fertilizers, pesticides, and herbicides. GMOs are not allowed in organic." More: https://rodaleinstitute.org

Book about **biointensive gardening**, How to Grow More Vegetables (and fruits, nuts, berries, grains and other crops) Than You Ever Thought Possible on Less Land Than You Can Imagine, by John Jeavons. In order to achieve these benefits, the biointensive method uses an eight-part integrated system of deep soil cultivation ("double-digging") to create raised, aerated beds; intensive planting; companion planting; composting; the use of open-pollinated seeds; and a carefully balanced planting ratio of 60% Carbon-Rich Crops (for compost production) 30% Calorie-Rich Crops (for food) and an optional 10% planted in Income Crops (for sale). Using these methods (decades of practice), John Jeavons says that 215 square feet with biointensive methods yields enough veg for one person.

Permaculture is an overall design/thinking strategy, that I have applied here, using Nature as our guide. There are online and in-person courses (about 12 days) called the, Permaculture Design Course, which I would recommend, even online with Geoff Lawton.

Biodynamic gardening, is another organic style of gardening, rooted in the work of philosopher and scientist Dr. Rudolf Steiner, whose 1924 lectures to farmers opened a new way to integrate scientific understanding with a recognition of spirit in nature.

A **Food forest** mimics a regular forest, with its various layers: ground cover, bushes, vines, small trees, canopy trees, etc., but it is planned to yield as much human food as possible. Dave Jacke book, Edible Forest Gardens, and other publications.

Other styles include: Foraging, Orchard and Medicinal gardens.

Grow Food on Roofs:

Most urban areas have thousands of acres of roof space suitable for food production. However, we must understand the technical requirements for this before going forward. This applies to access, roof covering, drainage, and if the joists or substructure are strong enough to hold up wet soil in raised beds, water storage, foot traffic, etc. Most roofs are designed to hold up only themselves and a large snow load, this is not sufficient for a garden. That doesn't mean it can't happen, just that we need to acknowledge what modifications are needed.

Brooklyngrangefarm.com.

Wicking Planters:

A great way to grow plants in dry climates, due to sub-soil watering with less evaporation. Also, in my case, I use them throughout the winter in my hoop house (polytunnel), most plants love the dampness, which being below the surface inhibits pest development. Depending on climate, the water level only needs replenishing every couple of weeks. Use a container deep enough to hold about 8 inches of soil with an extra 4-inch cavity below to act as a water reservoir. Shall we call it hydrosoil-ponics? Use weed-cloth to contain some soil that sits in the water, through the false bottom or whatever system you embrace, which then wicks upwards into the bulk of the soil. Place a pipe to facilitate filling the reservoir from the top.

Various methods to contain water below soil

Weed cloth pushed into hole allowing soil to sit in water and promote wicking

Cut top of tote to fit on wood base

Mid-winter harvest

Winter growing, hoop house filled with wicking planters

While replacing my 3 year top-surface plastic, I realized I could put chicken wire to reinforce it for snow load, while making the new plastic removable for summer growing. Chicken wire also keeps out the critters in summer

Closing the 'Anything Organic' Loop

There is no such thing as waste in nature because everything nature makes is organic, meaning something that once had life, and in its demise, becomes food for something else and we can do that: compost making, recycling food scraps, processing landscape biomass to make next year's soil. Closed loop. A few years ago, I was worried about peak oil, which has happened for easy-to-get oil; it's a downward supply from here on. But, actually, more acute, or just as, will be the need for soil, which is being lost to erosion, poisoning, degrading, etc., at an alarming rate. No soil, no people! 40% of food wasted world-wide in different parts of the system, depending on which nation you live in. 40% of landfills are organic or food waste – which produces methane as it breaks down – we need this to be processed and recycled into the living landscape. Not to mention freeing up some more room for all our other waste. It takes 800 years for nature to make an inch of soil from decomposing rocks! We can't work on that replenishment schedule. And there are no dinosaurs dropping manure outside our cave to use on our garden beds! Can you imagine? Phew! It's a good thing dinosaurs came before humans, contributing to soil buildup.

We cannot afford to lose any more soil, or its products, which can be recycled. With that in mind, in Permaculture, we have something called hugleculture – mound growing. Instead of sending our biomass: logs, twigs, branches, leaves, grass clippings, etc., to the landfill, process them into soil using the nitrogen carbon interaction. It takes a while, but see the pictures.

My under-counter kitchen waste container, which I take out to the compost heap when half-full

Hugle making on the left, a raised bed with top soil removed and branches laid, then covered with soil, grass clippings, then a harvest next year

Generally, gardeners think in terms of green stuff – nitrogen and brown stuff – carbon, this is a general rule. However, exceptions like coffee grounds supply nitrogen, great for the compost heap. When mixing these, they produce an accelerated decomposition reaction. A word about compost: true compost is not rotting matter. Compost 'happens' when the balance of nitrogen and carbon matter and moisture are just right; with enough mass, minimum about 1 cubic yard (1 cubic meter). This balance isn't super critical, but when it's right, the mass heats up to about 160 degrees F (71C), due to bacterial activity, not the sun. Basically, you get a bacterial civilization exploding for 14 days or so inside the pile and then it self-destructs (sound familiar?), and left a little longer, the finished product is compost – when all the pathogens, seeds, and original stuff has died and transformed and no longer looks like the original – that's compost. Without this bacterial explosion, you have rotting substances, which don't necessarily destroy seeds or pathogens. Rotting mass is still good for the garden, but it needs lots more time to break down. By adding a few inches of compost to a garden surface each year, it rejuvenates the soil. Know well the source ingredients of any compost you buy in case it contains herbicides that can be active for weeks and could affect your growing areas.

Another hugle above, at large scale they take years to break down, but the resulting biomass is amazing.
Using my rotary compost screener to refine the compost.

Nature In the Garden:
While we are redesigning our properties towards sustainability, we need to broaden our knowledge, awareness and attitude to include the millions of non-human others, then we will have gone beyond sustainability towards regenerative. Those non-human others actually make up the web of life that sustains us (biodiversity). It's under threat right now, so anything we can do to help rebuild it would be welcomed and actually comes under, enlightened self-interest. Consider the birds, critters, insects, biological pest management, pollinators, raptors, miniature wetlands, creature habitat, etc. There are micro-climates on your property (warm and cool spots which can be used to advantage), know the compass points and where the sun is in various seasons. You're creating your very own nature reserve, (see Prof. Doug Tallamay's:
https://homegrownnationalpark.org for more). And while we're at it, get parents together and convert school properties to nature reserves, designed and built with the input of children, so that we have space for outdoor classrooms and make education more interesting.

However, although we want to nurture the wildlife of our ecosystem, in urban environments it's a challenge. E.g., I had a skunk family living under my porch one spring/summer. Two adults and two children. They came out every night and foraged about, occasionally we interacted, which would be a problem with children or pets. So, this is something I don't want again. They stunk the place up with their poop and their interactions nightly with feral cats, making them fire off their awful smell, which is so strong you'd think they were under your bed! And the fanciful graphics I've seen of deer roaming our cities, is just that. Deer are spooked by their own poop falling on dried leaves, so they're not coming into town deliberately. Groundhogs can't be tolerated in the edible garden as they'll wipe out your efforts in a day. But we need to have semi-wild areas among human habitat, so they can eke out a living there, some work for architects to design such places, see my wall idea. Below sacrificing parsley plants at end of season for Swallowtail caterpillars.

Making a back-yard beehive, a great way to start a honey bee hive before going all in.
NOTE: Bees are vegetarians, wasps are carnivores, but they scoop up caterpillars.

Note on **food animals** in the urban garden. Every spring my local post office tweets loudly with the sound of chicken chicks that have been sent by the thousand, through the mail, to local residents, not all urban. In a garden six blocks away, there is a large wooden pigeon coup that has been there for 50 years. These are harvested for food. Poultry appears to be very doable in the urban setting, especially for eggs. And there are other small animals that can be raised also. I haven't covered this here as I have no exposure to it. I've been a vegetarian for 45 years, so it's hard for me to see the need and increased complications of raising creatures.

Trees In The FSN:

I love trees. Houses don't love trees. I've repaired houses for over 40 years and a tree close to a house, while giving shade, also gives its annual debris and root complications. This is not just the autumn leaves, but all year long. This promotes moss growth on the roof, gutters blocked with leaves (and rarely cleaned out in a timely manner), therefore water gushing over window-sills and side of the house, causing rot, and on into the basement. Wet basements are 99% caused by roof water – fact! The danger from falling trees is rare, except at the end of their lives and often triggered by a severe storm.

For the gardener, of course, shade isn't welcome in the food growing areas, and in the urban setting we don't really have enough room for large trees on our properties. They are in my street, but I noticed that many are about the same age, so, when they age out, many trees tend to get removed about the same time. Municipalities resist replanting because they have to dig up the sidewalk to plant them and then they will need management for the first few years. I'm always amazed that any tree can grow in the street, with its roots spreading below concrete sidewalks and tarred roads. Some of you may think that tree roots grow straight down and that's how they support themselves, and in the first few years of a tree's life there is a tap-root, but after a few years this withers and the lateral roots become the main support. Literally, these lateral roots grow out from the tree no deeper than 18 inches (45 cm) – Penn State, Master Gardener training. Why would they go deeper with no nutrition down there? So, when plumbers say the tree roots damaged the sewer pipe, that's not possible, because they're usually six feet (2 meters) down, the sewer pipe leaked or broke then the nutrition in the pipe wicked up into the soil and the roots followed it down. These lateral roots will also steal the nutrition from the great soil in your plant beds. (My cherry tree roots punched through an old bag of potting soil I left under my garden bench, completely engulfing it.) Unless you have a large enough property, large trees are not going to work for you. Of course, if you can accommodate large trees, you're going to benefit from growing your own fuel, building and craft materials and excess leaf debris that can help produce compost; not to mention supporting the local ecology, which could be extensive, hundreds of species of birds, moths, butterflies, insects and squirrels, etc. Coppicing a tree refers to the practice of cutting a tree back to the ground to encourage new growth. This is often done with willow trees to producing sticks for weaving craft projects or kindling. Pollarding is cutting or pruning the higher branches of a tree to produce various results, one might be favoring one branch to become a boat mast or lumber for a barn.

We want to make room for manageable fruit trees, which produce some shade and their debris should be left under the trees for their ongoing nutrition. Fruit trees prefer limited plants growing under them for best results.

I use a small shop vac, putting the cut top of a plastic bottle on the end of pipe, to vacuum pests off plants.

Succession:

"My garden has a mind of its own," said my neighbor. Turns out it does. "What?" It dreams of becoming a rain forest. "Na!" Yep! "How come?" Nature hates bear soil. "Why?" The wind blows it away and the rain erodes it. So, our 'friends' the weeds quickly grow to hold it in place. We all owe our lives to weeds! Note on grass: If you want great grass, don't cut it below 3 inches (7.5cm), the leaf is a solar panel that feeds the roots, below 3 inches the weeds can dominate, above 3, the grass will shade out the weeds – Penn State Master Gardener training.

As the soil holds and deepens, the small shrubs and bushes start growing. Succession has begun. Later, the small trees grow, shading out some of the first 'pioneer' plants, finally the big guys get going: black walnuts, oaks, etc., and many others. Large trees transpire (sweat), 300 plus gallons of water into the air every day in summer. This creates a dense, damp condition in the sky above them that can rain back on the forest, self-watering, living millennia, until fire or loggers arrive! We gardeners fight this process, that's why it's hard work – working against Nature.

That's why some people are planting forest gardens, or food forests. That's not a garden in a forest, but designing an edible forest, using all the layers down to some annual plants in the clearings, where the summer sun reaches. Using as many perennials as possible – fruit and nut trees, soft fruit bushes like blueberries, raspberries, vines like grape, kiwi, plus plants like asparagus and sunchoke, etc. It's hard to do this on a small property, but on larger ones we could establish food cornucopias for years to come.

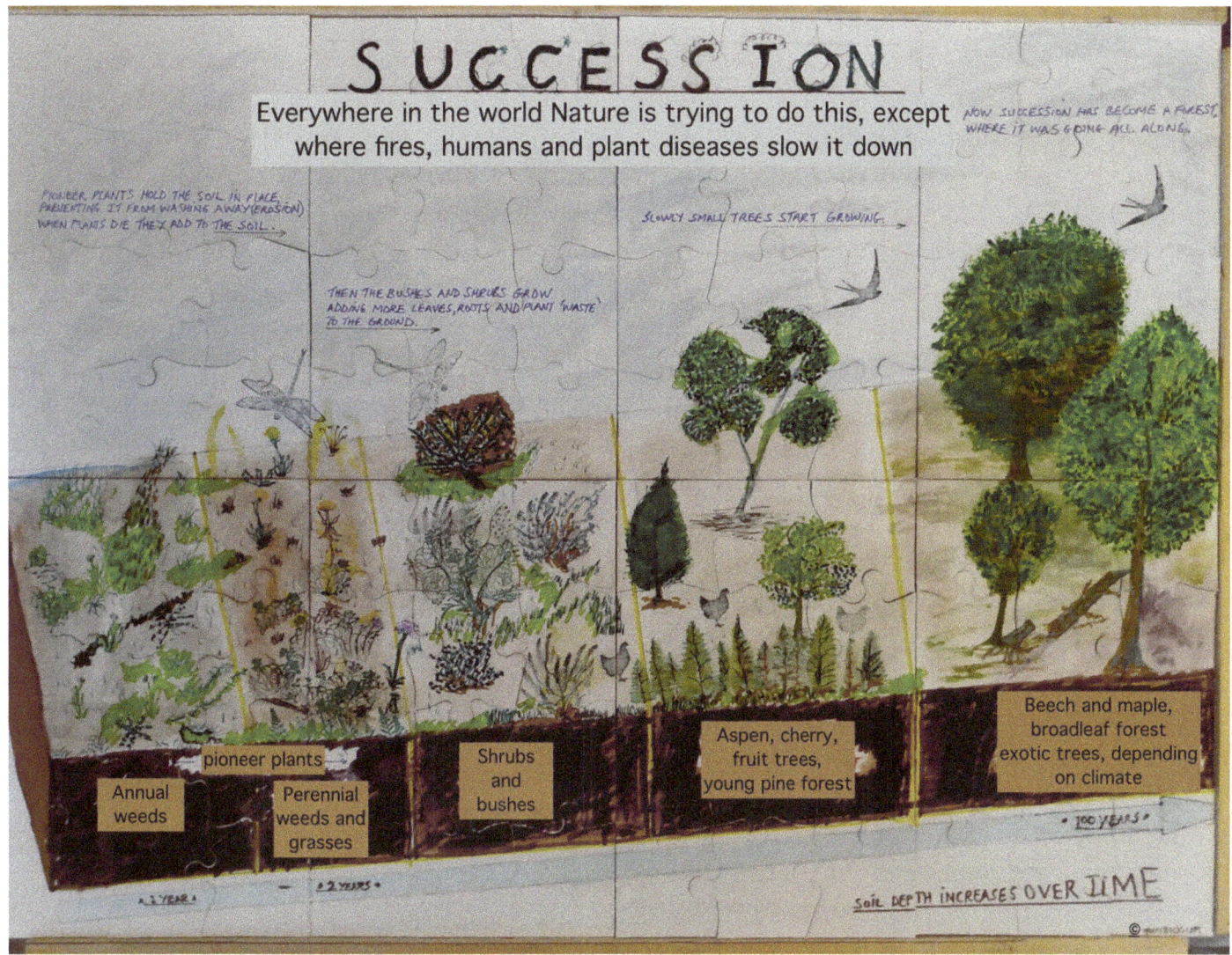

There is a lot of talk about planting only native plants, those that have co-evolved with the present ecology of a region, and in general that is correct. However, here in Pennsylvania apples and peaches are not native, but we wouldn't think of uprooting them. It's the same with things like bamboo, although there are some native varieties, the non-natives grow faster and larger, and if you're in need of an urgent barrier – behind your house on a slope, to prevent erosion from extreme weather effects – these can really help. They're also invasive, grow like hell, but that can be controlled. They are also a great resource for garden products – great business for some young person! So, it's best if we stay open and use our wisdom around such things.

(*Permaculture Principle:* Creatively use and respond to change: We can have a positive impact on inevitable change by carefully observing, and then intervening at the right time.)

SEEING NOT LOOKING – Soilnoia:
Soil anxious people. Clearly, a lot of tech bros and sisters, don't like soil. They're always trying to find non-soil ways to grow food. And I get it, soil is unpredictable, it contains billions of micro-organisms doing their thing, it doesn't like control, and it's non-linear. But, so-called, hydroponics, (water-works) sounds like a dream come true, except you need buildings that are heated, cooled and full of light, (part of the cost often ignored by the wizards trying to convince us it's a great thing). That means lots of energy just to run the building. Then, they pump water around to the plants and they grow. Hello, they never mention what's in the water: fossil fuel derived fertilizer/nutrients that you have to buy from a corporation. We may need interim systems of this nature under food supply-chain duress. So, let me put out a challenge, what would soil-ponics look like!?

Home-scale Aquaculture hesitancy: Fish feed from where? Water temperature, care for biology, initial setup, reliable electricity, (me being vegetarian, don't see the benefit, beans for protein easier to grow). Maybe in warmer climates (sub-tropical and tropical) where there is no fear of freezing under normal conditions. Commercial scale in oceans and fiords, but must farm as close to natural systems as possible, which means naturally wild nutrition levels also, otherwise sick fish.

Ultimately, for food security, we need to encourage agro-urban spaces, or agro-hoods, while re-localizing the entire food system – worldwide.

An historical note:
I know a 93-year-old lady who told me her father would come home from the steel mill, take his shotgun and head into the local wooded hillside, the woodlands were more extensive back then. He would return each evening with either a groundhog, opossum, squirrels, rabbit, etc., and hand them to the mother to cook for that night's dinner. She still works part-time at a local real estate firm, I know rabbits were a part of my diet when I was young – like any time, our future appetites will decide.

RAINWATER HARVESTING:

Can you use one or some of these rainwater harvesting strategies?

Let's say the average home roof is 1,000 square feet (93 square meters), not the internal area of the house, just the roof, looking down from the rain's point of view. For a one-inch (2.5cm) rainstorm, that's 625 gallons (2,366 liters) or about 12 average-size water barrels falling on the roof alone! Where I live, we get about 44 inches (112 cm) of rain annually, which would equal about 27,500 gallons (104,104 liters). According to my municipal water supply company, I use about 5-700 gallons a month, or 8,000 a year. If I had 3 teenage children, most of that roof water would be flowing through my house pipes for showers, toilets and washing machine! With a little design our pipes can be configured to do this. (1,000 square feet multiplied by 1", divided by 12 to get 83.33 cubic feet, multiplied by 7.48 gallons per cubic foot, equals approx. 625 gallons.)

(Permaculture Principle: Catch and store energy. By developing systems that collect resources when they are abundant, we can use them in times of need.)

Use and value renewable resources and services:

Make the best use of nature's abundance to reduce our consumptive behavior and dependence on non-renewable resources.

> 1,000 square feet (93 square meters) of roof, not the internal area of the house, just the roof, looking down from the rain's point of view. For a one-inch (2.5cm) rainstorm, that's 625 gallons (2,366 liters) or about 12 average-size water barrels falling on the roof alone! Where I live, we get about 44 inches (112 cm) of rain annually, which would equal about 27,500 gallons (104,104 liters). Can you use this?

Agriculture demands the most water, but industry is second, it's time they started harvesting vast amounts of rainwater, taking the 'pressure' off municipal supplies. Household uses for rainwater: Irrigation, utilitarian within the house, and drinking water. One of the best places to store water is in your soil, this will hydrate your land, replenish ground and subterranean water around you. Direct downspouts onto your land, pushing water out at least 4 feet from your foundation and not pointed towards the street. Know the slopes of ground around your house, including where it interfaces with neighboring properties, so that those aren't creating problems for you.

On larger properties, slow the flow, using berms (swales), not too high, on contour (90 degrees to slope) to prevent water loss and soil erosion from your property, (see 'A' frame picture). This helps reduce flooding, regenerates wells, aquifers and hydrates your land so that droughts have less impact. When the runoff is on contour, it hits the berm equally along its length without causing washout.

Hydrated land, by design, not effort, on right

Catch-a-raindrop fitted to downspout with holes drilled in hose.

New berm on contour. Rain accumulates equally along length, preventing washout in one area.

Put A frame on a level surface like your kitchen floor, mark where the string stops, that's level. On landscape, when the string hits the mark, that's level, mark the ground position for berm and move along the ground.

Different size tanks on the property can serve different purposes. We direct downspouts and gutters toward them, putting first-flush systems (see picture) that allow us to redirect a little water that may contain debris from the roof. Large tanks like 1,000 gallons (4' x 4' x 8') can be used for irrigation or emergency supplies. Regular garden barrels are around 50 gallons! This stored water can be gravity fed around the garden using a hose or watering can. A small pond pump can be dropped into the tank to supply pressure through the hose, which is useful in some circumstances. These small pumps can also be used to move ground level water supplies to higher levels, but check lift rate before buying.

I use rainwater for drinking (10 years). Irrigation water is OK from shingle or wooden shake roofs, but a metal surface produces a cleaner supply for personal consumption. In an emergency it is clean enough to drink, but I filter it using a Life Saver five-gallon jerry can.

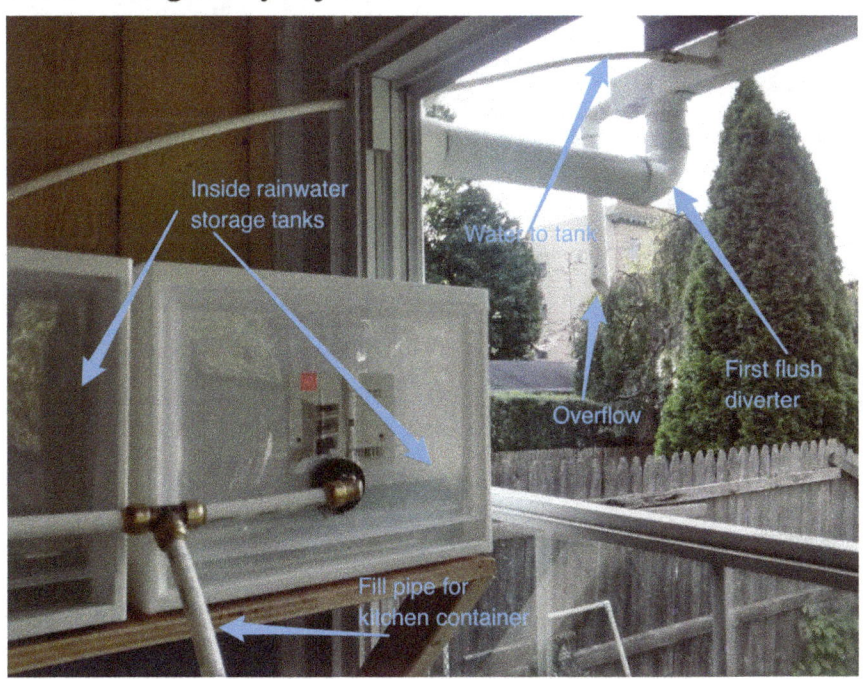

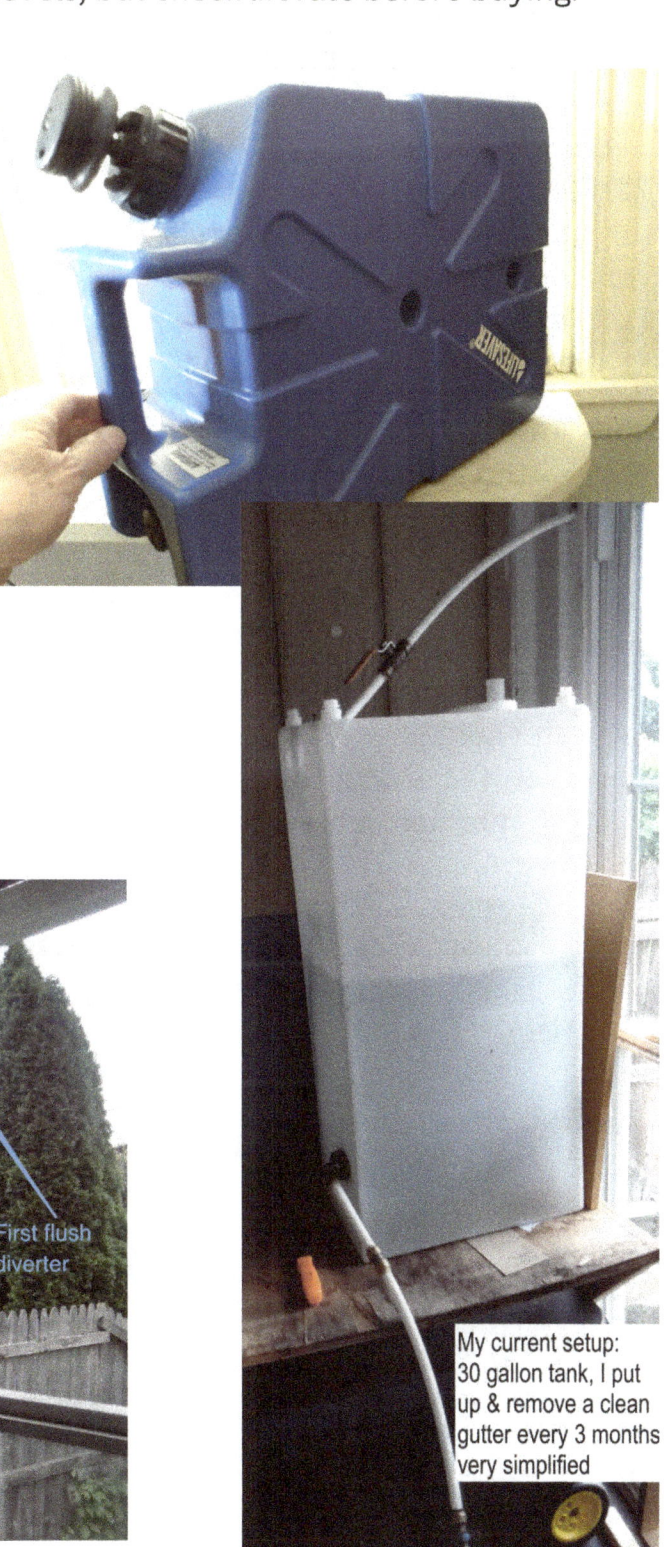

My current setup: 30 gallon tank, I put up & remove a clean gutter every 3 months very simplified

What has the California drought got to do with me?

New York Times, 5/21/15:

The average American consumes more than **300 gallons** of California water each week by eating food that was produced there.

Sliver of avocado = 4.1 gallons
Two ounces of rice = 15.1 gals.
16 almonds = 15.3 gals.
4 broccoli florets = 2.2 gals.
1 slice of bread = 3.2 gals.
1/3 head of lettuce = 4.1 gals.
1.75 ounce of turkey = 21.75 gals (not free-range)
1.75 ounce of beef = 86 gals. (not grass fed)
1 x 8oz glass of milk = 35.75 gals.

Important note: shallow ground water wells, say 10-20 feet are no longer safe in dense building areas because they could be contaminated, but maybe OK for irrigation. Also, if you have a property with a deep well, during power cuts there's no supply, so, consider putting a fifty-gallon tank in the attic, feeding one cold faucet somewhere in the house, then you'll know that during a power cut, you're good for 50 gallons on that faucet. Only once or twice a growing season do I run out of irrigation water with about 300 gallons stored in the garden. I use the most economical mosquito-bits containing, bacillus thuringiensis (BT), in my irrigation rainwater containers to prevent mosquito larvae throughout the warmer months.

Tip: If you vacate the house in winter or any long periods, turn off main water supply, then, if there is a problem, only the pipe contents leak out, no gushing under pressure.

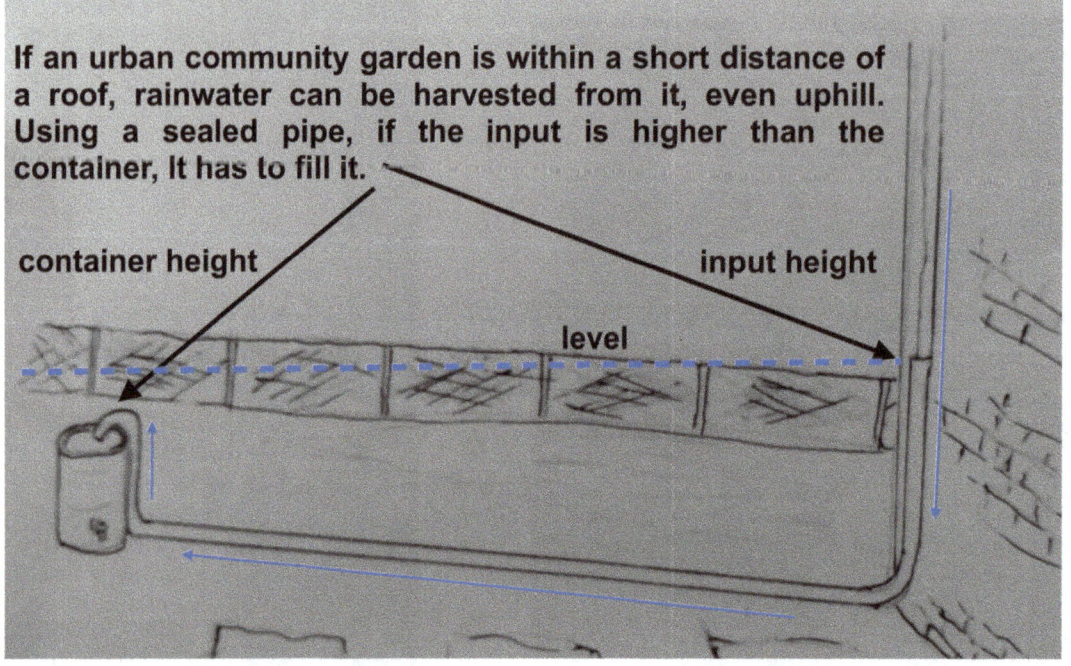

GO DEEP FOR SUSTAINABLE ANSWERS:

"...the key to autonomy is that a living system finds its way into the next moment by acting appropriately out of its own resources." Francisco Varela.

I think, because of the advantage of fossil fuels, our non-industrial innovative thinking has become lazy. For instance, a customer of mine had a garage in her basement, at the bottom of a sloped driveway. If it rained enough, it flooded, and then came the remnants of hurricane Ida. Yikes! So, next time I visited to paint the kitchen, she took me out back, saying, "you're a sustainability guy, solve this for me." First, I suggested we install pumps in a cavity under the driveway. "No pumps," she said, "the power went off during Ida." Let's do a drain and reroute the water around the house. "But to where?" she asked, "my neighbor's property?" I looked around, she was surrounded on all sides by other properties. She had considered doing away with the garage, having the basement wall built up in front of where the door was, then landscaping the area to omit the driveway. Cost, about $35,000, and the loss of driveway and garage. She said, "it's got to be passive, non-mechanized; imagine, I'm away, the power goes out, there's no one to supervise it, but it doesn't flood. I'll pay you just to give me a remedy." So, I worked out how much area, and therefore volume of rainwater was contributing to the problem. I kept thinking of solutions and then eliminating them, because they needed some kind of babysitting. Then, eventually, going really deep, boom, there it was.

The customer came out and I explained it. We need to dig a hole in front of the garage door deep enough to hold a concrete tank 4' x 4' x 8' wide (120 x 120 x 240cm), that's about 1,000 gallons (4,000 liters). Then below that put 2 feet of gravel, so at least a 6' deep hole by 4' x 8'. On the surface of the driveway, we need a large commercial street drain that allows the water to drop without getting blocked with debris, so no fine mesh. She was a practical person and realized this could do it. "Do you want to do the job?" she asked. No, too much for me. "Shall I call my plumber?" No, that's not the person, wait, um, who can do this? I know, it's the septic tank people, this is their work, only make sure they break holes in the bottom of the tank so the water can soak away into the ground through the gravel. I made a rough sketch for her to show a contractor if she wanted to get prices. I figured this design could handle even a hurricane Ida sized storm.

Anyway, I finished my kitchen painting and didn't return there for a couple of weeks. When I did, the customer said, "Come out back, I want to show you something. Look, how about that?" There was this huge drain grate in the driveway and I looked into this massive hole. Oh, my God, you did it already. "Yes, I did, I told you I'm keen to sell this place. The contractor had a bell-shaped concrete tank with no bottom, that's what you're looking at, about the size you recommended, plus the gravel. Backhoe, trucks, a small crane, quite an operation." Wow! How much? "About $12,000," she said, and I must have looked surprised. "I'm delighted, a third of the cost of the alternative, and I get to keep my garage and driveway." When I gave her my next bill, she gave me a bonus. We can do this. And that's an example of what I mean by going deep for the least industrial-dependent sustainable design solutions.

COMMUNITY:

Modern life: We're educated for a job, only to be self-reliant in an industrial or service job and production society, working for money, becoming buyers not makers, dependent not independent. Our life products are bought from corporations (often from low wage countries) – not self-generated. We're dependent on the health of the stock market and centralized distribution from non-local sources with just-in-time supply chains. You could be monetarily wealthy – but left empty-handed in a crisis. What good is it having a million in the bank when there's little food to buy in the marketplace?

So, how to disengage from reliance on modernity and satisfy basic needs from self-reliant sources/methods? Where are the effective pressure points in your life where you could start living differently without reverting to arduous, primitive lifestyle options? Currently, any move away from modernity helps Nature, your life, though not immediately apparent, and the planet. Try to pass all future decisions through the self-reliant, sustainable, regenerative focus. Do you need to skill-up? What knowledge or skills do you need? Do you need to move? What do you need in order to change? There are two drivers here: sustainability and a need to pivot away from total reliance on modernity. Why? Because committed Sustainers think that bumps in the road of modernity are inevitable and we want to reduce their impact on our lives. So, it's important to build alternative support scaffolds. These initiatives could help social cooperation flourish, leading us all to enjoy more community connections, which most people do enjoy. This includes building an alternative network of supply, before there is an emergency, e.g., supporting local food production and distribution, continuously, not just in a crisis. There could be people in your network with whom you barter and swap. Understand and get clear about your basic needs provisioning. Make a list, include medications. Sometimes folks mention they want to get 'off the grid.' They usually mean dependance on electricity. But life isn't that simple now, consider: food, water, medications, electric supply, natural gas, petroleum, transport, communications, financial system, plumbing/waste disposal, education, entertainment, spiritual, social, family – a bit more going on in and around our 'caves' nowadays than 10,000 years ago. "Sustainability is an active condition of problem solving," (Professor Joseph Tainter, Collapse of Complex Societies). Our formal learning teaches reliance for goods and employment on modernity and its complex systems. Informal learning, like this book, hopes to give us useful knowledge that isn't necessarily in the formal learning environment. Therefore, it's private learning, a can-do approach with an empowering psychological benefit, I think. Even better when practiced in connection with others. Also: sewing circles, arts, crafts, writing groups, local gardeners, etc.

HEALTH:

I think, if we're consuming more than 15% from corporate processed food sources, we're committing suicide on the instalment plan! You want to recognize the real food original ingredients on your plate to signal a healthful meal. Consider the nutrition needed for children's brains. "If a child is overweight, his or her life expectancy may be reduced by 10 to 20 years." A review of multiple studies cited in the book Food Fix, page 141, by Mark Hyman, MD. Exercise, psychological benefits, nourishment: these FSN actions improve health through movement, organic plants and plant awareness. Eco – trauma healing: I think that embedded in all modern people are the effects of ecological grief, (Global Alliance for the Future of Food, P.15) therefore we need nature therapy which, properly applied, the Future Sustainable Neighborhood can satisfy. Research the herbs that are known to help alleviate the negatives of whatever health condition you have, and incorporate them into your diet. According to many experts 80% of our health problems can be mitigated with smart lifestyle choices. Although we're all subject to hunger, illness, aging and death, by making wise choices, we have some control over hunger and illness; and by extension, maybe aging and death.

HUMAN WASTE:
We either have municipal water and sewerage, or a septic sewer system and well-water. It is very rare for municipal systems to become unusable. However, some septic systems use a pump to get the waste to the underground septic tank (good to know if your system has this), and well-water needs electricity to draw it up and into the house. So, in an emergency, two 5-gallon buckets, one for poop, one for pee, keep separate. Use sawdust, soil, kitty litter, etc. for both. Pre-dig a small trench in the garden to put the stuff and keep a shovel to cover each deposit. Or, if an enclosure can be placed around the trench, go directly in the garden. This would be a rare need, hasn't happened to me in all my years. Use stored rainwater for cleaning buckets, yourself and flushing toilets. In a natural cycle, as with all the other animals, our personal waste would be recycled through the soil, but the municipal sewer system interrupts this, sending it down rivers to the ocean. All our food came from the soil, so our waste is now lost soil, never to return, and it's a massive amount. There may come a time when we can't afford to do this. (It's estimated that the waste from livestock could provide over half the fertilizer needs of the world. At present this is not used at any scale and contributes to land, water-ways and ocean degradation and pollution. It's hard to establish when the fossil fuel industry has a lock on making nitrogen fertilizer from natural gas.)

MISCELANIOUS:
Remember: nature loves you.
My 93-year-old neighbor used to have a favorite secret spot in the fields near our town, where every spring he and a few others would go to pick wild broccoli rabe. None of that exists today due to Agricide farming with herbicides. As a child, he was also fed scrambled eggs with dandelion leaves. The leaves can be a bit bitter, so use sparingly, and best picked young, they're as nutritious as any other vegetable. I maintain that if you're of European descent, your ancestors probably avoided starvation at some point by eating the humble dandelion leaf – first up in spring during what was called the 'gap month,' between the end of winter stored food and the new plant growth.
If you have to dump something toxic, make the effort and do it the best way recommended to avoid pollution. Never put toxic waste down drains in the street, they usually flow to the nearest stream or river; better to flush it, believe it or not, because the waste water plant is more likely able to process it.

SEEING NOT LOOKING – Emergy:

Howard T. Odum began the perceptive study of energy that became known as the concept of Emergy. From what I understand, Emergy assesses all the various energy flows and energy conversions required to manifest a product, much of which is hidden from view. Nate Hagens often says economists are "energy blind," in fact this blindness is often very convenient to many players in the manufacturing world. Emergy is complicated, the consumption of unseen energy of course also means unseen pollution costs and accounting tricks, hidden from view. By understanding the Emergy of our actions, we have the big picture view, which could lead to better use of resources. It seems to me that the pace of the modern world would rather overlook these subtleties. An example is that for every small product we discard, there are magnitudes of resources, unseen, to produce it. All this effort is discarded along with the product. Nevertheless, this puts stress on the Earth Systems: geosphere, biosphere, cryosphere, hydrosphere, and atmosphere, and whether we address this or not, the 'system knows,' so watch out! What corporation, politician or religious authority ever cared about this?

FSN BUSINESS OPPORTUNITIES:

You'd like to start a neighborhood bakery, but can't afford the equipment up front? How about we apply the CSA, community supported agriculture model to neighborhood businesses? The CSA customer pays a farmer up front for the farmer's produce grown throughout the year. This helps farmers establish their business needs from the get go. Applied to a bakery, an owner could find and charge 200 customers, willing to pay maybe $300 up front, for weekly loaves throughout the year. This would allow the business owner to set up the business, buy ovens, store remodeling, etc., with $60,000 financing, not to mention all the other revenue from other purchases from the store. CSB, community supported bakery, or whatever!

Jane Jacobs, in her book, Cities and the Wealth of Nations, speaks of, import substitution or replacement: when a region begins making products that were previously imported from elsewhere and how that increases the wealth of such places. Possibly re-localizing the food system and other initiatives could be interpreted in this way.

Personal conservation (less trinket desire), home cooking and home production are sources of income and could provide satisfaction and empowerment from self-provisioning. I also think our children's education will be enhanced by FSN. FSN may lead to enhanced local economic development.

Local neighborhood business opportunities

The Household Economy:

Question: What is the household economy? These Household Economy Entrepreneurs suggests a new name and I'm calling us **Hentrepreneurs!**

Answer: The household economy has been almost lost to modern people who have become known as consumers, where corporations make and supply everything. North Americans used to be the workers in those corporations producing the goods – that is no longer the case. We are now mostly post-industrial. Most manufacturing is now overseas and our population works mainly in the service industries that support the marketing, sale and distribution of goods, and the public sector.

The consumer economy really got going in the 1920s to maximize the consumption of over-producing factories. Meanwhile, the household economy ran alongside the industrial economy. Before industrialization, the Western world was almost 100% a household economy, much like two-thirds of the rest of the world today. There are two kinds of household economy: 1) The closed household economy which are the benefits of the collected efforts contained within the household that do not leave the household, and 2) the open household economy where the benefits of the collected efforts may be bartered or sold for monetary gain. Let's explore the Open Household Economy.

Question: Why do we need to return to a household economy?
Answer: Some people now realize that it's time to rebuild the household economy – especially for lower income and less educated people whose jobs were more dependent on a manufacturing base.

Other reasons may include:

- Larger percentage of unemployed among certain populations
- Lack of job opportunities in a de-industrialized economy
- No-growth, steady-state economy due to world economy (marks a new time in history for Western nations, never been here before)
- Many fiscal slopes ahead for Western economies: unfunded pensions, expensive crumbling infrastructure, lower tax revenues, lack of political and corporate will to plan for this future due to causing marketplace uncertainty, threatening the legacy providers (status quo)
- Unknown impacts from climate change to North America and the rest of the world, we may see climate change refugees, some arriving on our shores, but also vacating the desert states due to water shortages
- Energy supplies will almost certainly be more expensive as supplies reduce and demand increases (3 billion people in India and China want to become middle class, and will strive for this)
- A new group of unemployed are on the horizon: they will be known as the techno-unemployed, the people put out of work by robots, AI, etc., this wave is hitting along with the unemployed from the digital disruptive innovations
- The availability of money as currency in the economy will shrink

- **Question:** What does the 21st century household economy look like?
- **Answer:** Many factors determine it. For example, geography. The Japanese version may look different to the North American. Local communities may have varying needs for products or services such as a farming community versus an urban one. How about the income levels of communities? Some may buy a locally made item to support an emerging artisan, or because they want a hand-made item instead of a factory mass-produced one for that particular function. This would create very interesting products.

- It may seem like a lot of trouble to start a household initiative if your job hasn't been affected, or you draw down a great salary, and perhaps have little extra time for these activities. However, some countries in Europe already experience high unemployment, the U.S. true numbers may not reflect the reality. With under-employed households an extra couple of thousand dollars a year is greatly appreciated. Indeed, with the lack of jobs we may all need small, multiple streams of income as the world changes. Of course, these household-income products can also be bartered.

- At the moment our communities and regions are very vulnerable to the outer shocks from the world economy insecurities, from food production (6% of our food is grown within the 8 counties around Philadelphia), lack of preparation around climate change, to uncertain energy prices and supplies; this all leads to the smarter initiative of re-localizing our basic needs worldwide. If every community is locally sustainable and resilient, then everyone in the world is protected.

Ideas that may constitute the new household income initiatives in North America - or they could be called micro-industries:

Food system:

- Small homesteads producing locally grown fresh fruit and vegetables for local markets (this will further stimulate more producers, farmers, processors, markets, produce swaps, storage facilities, soil services, etc.
- The food initiative is a signature activity that can stimulate so many other initiatives:
- Food processing like canning and dehydrating
- Home bakeries
- Locally cooked food distribution for busy families who want to eat home-cooked food
- Specialty food preparation
- Education around food production
- All services like composting, vermiculture, soil delivery, garden installations, growing structures
- Greenhouse construction for extended season growing initiatives
- Micro-greens and sprout production
- Soy dairies
- Plant nursery
- Fruit orchards and fruit products
- Productive edible garden design

Crafts/products:

- Pottery
- Custom wood products
- Garden structures
- Sewing repair
- Short run clothing manufacture
- Specialized clothing manufacture
- Repurposed clothing manufacture
- Recycled tools, shoes/boots, car parts, clothing accessories
- Knitting/wool products
- Picture framing
- Re-purposed anything
- Soap making
- Specialized paper products
- Toys
- Art products: paintings of local views, portraits, etc.
- Bamboo products

Home-based Education:

- Math, reading and writing tuition
- Skills training (re-skilling for new challenges)
- Specialized subjects like Permaculture, Draft-busting, Health-related cooking, Child rearing, etc.
- Music studio
- Tuition on how to set up a household business
- Home schooling

Services:

- Child care
- Hairstylist
- Incomplete lists, add your own ideas.

Although many of us are very concerned about food production and energy shortages, other complex systems affect the Hentrepreneur. These categories need a sustainable framework: food, shelter, water, clothing, transport, energy, economic system, education, law, security, waste disposal, culture, community, spirit, belonging, localization, communication, innovation/experimentation, health, and diversity.
Let's not forget that the financial system has already collapsed several times in recent history with dire consequences. The Hentrepreneur is defending against this system by default.

1) Less dependence on the money system, mainly due to home manufacture of our own needs and goods that are barter-able;
2) Less dependence on the health-care system, mainly due to consumption of higher quality food, if growing your own is part of your effort; and more consciousness in general about what to eat (I think we can scientifically say now that modern corporate edible substances, products referred to as 'food' by these industries) are in fact detrimental to human health because they have been engineered to use cheap subsidized ingredients without regard to nutrition content and also manipulated to be addictive. If the Hentrepreneur can find an extended community of like-minded people, one's mental health is probably going to benefit, not to mention the empowerment benefit of being pro-active, alleviating thoughts of hopelessness. (Consider the synergy of the different skills within the community that can save us money, put more expertise at our fingertips, helping to solve day-to-day (even complex) problems.
3) Less dependent on worldwide industrial manufacture, mainly due to the ability to repair and self-manufacture.

"Use your resources to make wealth, don't sell them to make money." Odum. Meaning: If you have trees don't sell them, use them to make furniture and sell that.

Conclusion:

In future there may be less financial slack in the system. The modest income generated by bartering or selling a few products from a household- businesses could be a lifeboat. Lower income people are often more innovative and resourceful than wealthier folk because their resources and wealth are limited. Indeed, fashion designers have been known to scour low-income neighborhoods for innovative ideas, and new music forms often bubble up there. In nature it is at the edge of ecosystems where you see the most activity and biodiversity – it is the same in human culture. The unemployed or under-employed could become a new edge. Let's find a way for everyone to contribute, be valued and involved; including 'informal' populations. For instance, in my town we have an electric arc metal furnace, so some people use their trucks to pick up waste metal products put out on garbage collection days, hauling it to the scrap yards for a little extra pocket change, better recycled than ending up in the landfill.

Encouraging the **Open Household Economy** could lead to more robust neighborhood and regional economies, reducing financial stress, with less needs from the global economy. This makes our local environ more sustainable, resilient to worldly shocks that we don't control and even regenerative.

A surprisingly good re-use of old jeans, a garden/toolbelt   Upcycling

ABOUT TIME AND LABOR:

In my own life, I've seen the need to free myself from the tyranny of efficiency. Don't let that little voice in your head say you're going too slow, or by using machines it will be faster. Choose the joy of human labor and effort. We may need to adjust our attitude, if only to be more in sync with nature.

Amory Lovins, co-founder of the Rocky Mountain Institute: "We don't need any novel technology, we need smarter design."

1 horsepower | 300 horsepower

SEEING NOT LOOKING – Systems Thinking

Do you have an accurate understanding of the world you inhabit? System: "A set of elements or parts that is coherently organized and interconnected in a pattern or structure that produces a characteristic set of behaviors, often classified as its 'function' or 'purpose'," codified by Donella Meadows and others, see book: Thinking In Systems. In other words, full-on holistic thinking. This should be taught in high schools.

Example: What happens around the creation, or birth, of a bird? Can a bird just come into existence? Well, the normal way this happens is through an older female bird who has been inseminated by an older male bird. Ah, so this new bird is dependent on the existence of birds before it and a predatory system that didn't render its ancestors extinct. That means there has to be a support system for those birds in the form of: food supply, conducive weather, habitat material – trees, bushes, twigs, etc., possibly a community of bird species to which it belongs. When does that support system need to be in place for the birth of the new bird? Two years, 5, 20, 100, 10,000, 70,000 years?

Now the bird has to live, find a partner, reproduce, find thousands of insects to feed its children in the nest. It can't feed them seeds because they're too dry and the babies would choke and dehydrate. A bird can't carry water, but the moisture in the insects' bodies fulfills this need. They have to deal with our noisy world that has forced birds to sing louder in order to find mates. In urban areas, the nights flooded with artificial light, stresses out the wild creatures large and small, with little choice but to struggle on.

What about the disposal of the bird when it dies? If no animals were disposed of by nature, the world would be continually knee deep in dead critters and no plant matter could grow under their carcasses. (In fact, if worms, termites, ants, etc., didn't clean up falling debris from other plants, that would result in reduced plant growth, and reduced animal existence, also.) So, when the bird falls to its death, the billions of microbes, extent in the soil, spread throughout its body, slowly decomposing it; while the carrion beetles, rarely seen, that live subterranean, come to the surface to devour the carcass, unseen, from its underside – the true recyclers. Meanwhile, its feathers blowing through the grass, get picked up by other birds for nesting material.

Everything we do is contained within systems like this. Whether involving nature, our businesses, or our so-called mundane actions. The shoes we ware are made 12,000 miles from where we live with materials sourced from thousands of miles from where they're manufactured, etc. No wonder some business decisions that managers make don't pan out as expected, they haven't considered the whole system. Nothing we make or do is done in isolation.

QUOTES: from Designing Regenerative Cultures, by Daniel Wahl

"Along with increased diversity and resilience, increases in bioproductivity, ecosystems functions, social cohesion, collaboration and wellbeing are all indications of positive change in socio ecological systems and an increased capacity to respond to disruptions." Page 121.

"Rather than forcing a natural world separate from us to fit our human needs, as the narrative of separation would have us do, we have to fit-in as a species that has a lot to learn from the rest of nature in trying to discern which design solutions better serve the whole system." Page 153.

PERMACULTURE has 3 Ethics: Earth Care, People care, Fair share (Share surplus)
And 12 or more Permaculture Principles in the Garden:

1. Observe and interact: By taking the time to engage with nature we can design solutions that suit our particular situation.

2. Catch and store energy: By developing systems that collect resources when they are abundant, we can use them in times of need.

3. Obtain a yield: Ensure that you are getting truly useful rewards as part of the work that you are doing. 3 benefits from each action.

4. Apply self-regulation and accept feedback: We need to discourage inappropriate activity to ensure that systems can continue to function well.

5. Use and value renewable resources and services: Make the best use of nature's abundance to reduce our consumptive behavior and dependence on non-renewable resources.

6. Produce no waste: By valuing and making use of all the resources that are available to us, nothing goes to waste.

7. Design from patterns to details: By stepping back, we can observe patterns in nature and society. These can form the backbone of our designs, with the details filled in as we go.

8. Integrate rather than segregate: By putting the right things in the right place, relationships develop between those things and they work together to support each other.

9. Use small and slow solutions: Small and slow systems are easier to maintain than big ones, making better use of local resources and producing more sustainable outcomes.

10. Use and value diversity: Diversity reduces vulnerability to a variety of threats and takes advantage of the unique nature of the environment in which it resides.

11. Use edges and value the marginal: The interface between things is where the most interesting events take place. These are often the most valuable, diverse and productive elements in the system.

12. Creatively use and respond to change: We can have a positive impact on inevitable change by carefully observing, and then intervening at the right time.

Permaculture offers a decision-making framework using ecological principles to help design sustainable human communities. It's whole-systems thinking. What does that mean? Systems thinking focuses on the relationships among different parts and the synergy that emerges from these relationships. It's how the parts come together to make a greater whole. This is the key to sustainable living, as opposed to 'silo' thinking, where the focus is on just one part of the system. (More: https://holmgren.com.au)

SEEING NOT LOOKING – My 1500 CE., U.S. landscape muse:

Apparently, inhabitants of the Middle East had ecologically trashed the region by about 10,000 years ago, so they had to do agriculture to support themselves, and then, that spread to Europe. If they had taken care of the ecology, as the Turtle Island (U.S.) Indigenous people did, then widespread agriculture would not have been necessary, for they knew that they were living in their pantry, and so didn't trash it. Therefore, they could just walk out of their shelters and choose from two hundred edible plants in the neighborhood – imagine – that's why I think, gatherer/hunter, not hunter/gatherer is more accurate; you're not going to chase animals when all that nourishment grows on the vine in front of you. But what if you decided you'd like some meat, well how about some duck or fish for breakfast? Turtle Island was so abundant in the year 1500 of the common era (CE).

What would you think the keystone animal species was back then? You might think of something big like the wolf or bears, but in my opinion, from what I've read, it was the lowly beaver. There were billions of them back then. These little rivers that now flow through our towns were never like that back then. They were spread out all over the landscape. The beavers dammed every river, tributary, stream, in the country, they couldn't help themselves, it's what they do. Basically, much of the U.S. was a wetland with fish everywhere, clouds of foul, and large predators hoping to feed on the abundance. What we see of our landscape today is close to desertification compared to back then. The Europeans thought the Indigenous people were backward because they hardly did agriculture and they hadn't developed metal tools. They didn't need them! Agriculture, is a failure. The European ignorance was such that they could not discern the subtlety of how the Native Turtle Islanders lived with Nature – not imposing themselves on it. The Europeans set about killing off the beavers so that people in Europe could make hats and clothes from the pelts. They denuded the land of trees to smelt their iron production... and on and on. And this "culture" they have spread all over the Earth. Hence, a planet facing multiple natural tipping points, plus 6 out of 9 Planetary Boundaries already crossed. (Planetary Boundary Framework, Stockholm Resilience Center).

SEEING NOT LOOKING – It's Enough

We are fundamentally 'animals in a landscape,' that's all. For millions of years, as our bodies changed, we shared our lives with all the other creatures. Imagine yourself in that natural state. The construct of this modern world is an invention of our big brains, and could take the form of a million different versions. But now, many modern people live like a new species, locked in their skulls and electronic devices, while roaming sub-terranean shopping malls with artificial light, food and atmosphere; it's time to emerge above ground and seek to understand and join the community of life on Mother Earth.

So, to have a satisfying life as an animal, we need food, shelter and clothing, just like the rest of biology. I had a spiritual teacher who used to say, "If you have these three, you cannot say you are poor."

Adult humans have the metabolic need of about 2,000 calories a day to live, the operating level of a 100-watt light bulb, according to physicist Geoffrey West, (episode 117, TheGreatSimplification.com). And when really active, this climbs by a factor of 2-3 times, the same as all other mammals. However, the external metabolism needed to run each industrialized modern life, is equivalent to about 11,000 watts, which would be the energy used by 12 elephants; and yet, we're still incapable of saying, "I have enough."

PART TWO: THE WHYS?

The Great Dilemma – A message from Nature:

"Will the future story be egalitarian and a soft landing; or dystopian and a hard landing? You decide, it's in your hands."

Picture a benevolent force, life supporting, threatened by the very life it's trying to support. What should it do? What if I told you that I, Nature, am that force and you, the only species that reads letters, self-named, homo-sapiens (wise human), who is currently devolving into homo-consumere (consumer human), are that threat?

What am I to do? I am not allowed to claim sentience, according to you. But I have 3 ½ billion years of research and development (R&D), you would think I'd know something. I make your existence possible, but you have not facilitated my thriving, in fact quite the opposite. Do I have feelings? Cut a tree and see if it 'bleeds' and then heals. Crowd a plant and see if it doesn't bend in another direction, to bathe in the sun. Watch a lizard warm itself in the sun, (it can't work a coffee maker, I'll grant you that). See the animals nurture their babies and children. Give me a break, before I have to put the brakes on you, which you'll call wrath, and in your blindness, you won't see it as benevolence.

You were given so many rights. You could use Nature to your heart's content. But you don't have the right to destroy it, which is the worry now. Within limits I can endure you, but now you have passed them. What I am about to say will be difficult for some of you to hear, but we can observe that the Creator (omnipresent, omnipotent, omniscient, uncreated, and not a sky God), also has a tremendous tolerance towards Its creations. But in the end, the totality of Its creation to support all life, is more precious than any individual creature. Now, because you are sacrificing the Earth's biosphere on the altar of rampaging consumerism, not basic needs, including your unwillingness to change behavior in so many other areas, you are positioning yourselves to become a sacrificial element.

So, here's the thing. Within Me, Nature, there are tipping points, evolutionarily set to save Me (and therefore by extension, save you also), as you are dependent on Me, not Me on you. They go off when the planetary boundaries, as some call them, are passed. I've been trying to hold these together. But you're determined to surpass them – and then some. I'm so interconnected that when one tips, there will likely be a domino effect – you'll be very unhappy, pulling out that wrath-card again. Please! Sorry to blame the victim, but this will be your doing, not Ours.

However, get this – something else has come on the screen, as it were, I can use that word now, just a few decades ago that wouldn't have meant anything; ah, but you're not concerned with the long view. Because of my 3 ½ billion years of R & D, you should study how I do things and use that as your guidance, but you're too arrogant.

Oh well, as I was saying, this something else, other than My tipping points, is your regional conflicts. Now, they're not new, how many have I witnessed? Please, don't get me started. In the past, though, they happened, then fizzled. But now it's a whole new ball game, you're global, just like I've always been. And you've never had such a complex society, phew! And, like Me, all your systems are interconnected, dependent on each other, so many moving parts, so if one of your regionals goes ballistic, I can use that phrase, right? Now you've got the domino effect also, like me. But unlike me, I've got redundancy, resilience and time built in, you don't have that, you're sitting ducks.

Now, here's the thing. If a regional conflict goes ballistic, with everyone taking sides and pitching in, then it's global. Oh boy, you know what that means? Your modern world goes belly up in record time, what a year that will be! I'm not suggesting you'll go extinct, but… you won't like this scenario, *"People get ready, there's a train comin',"* do you know that song? No matter. The odd thing about this scenario, is that it may preempt My tipping points. Good for Us, but probably tougher on you, although you are part of Us. Now there's an irony!

You see, the cleverness is with you, you're just not utilizing it. You don't accept Our feedback: extreme weather events, warming planet faster than any time in Our recent story. Some of you know that systems give feedback. If you don't take note of these and make adjustments, then the systems will adjust themselves, and this you don't like.

Perhaps, instead of moving in slow motion, which is My nature, I should speed things up to give you a shock. This appears to be part of your collective blockage in not adjusting your lifestyles. This is the thing, you see, We are not mean. But, I'm thinking, maybe My compassion is being misconstrued.

So, that's where We're coming from, and what's the dilemma? You're damned if you do, and damned if you don't. What? It's funny, it occurred to Me, the sooner you do the ballistic regional conflict thing, the sooner I can get on with healing, that's if you don't go nuclear, then it might be game-over. Well, probably 'funny' isn't the right word. But you've got a lot of sub-human leadership in the world right now. This happens from time to time, but at the wrong time, like now, that's double jeopardy.

Meanwhile, here are some 'down-to-earth' ways to help Me. Within these the dilemma becomes more apparent and 'why' We need a sustainable neighborhood.

1. Two worlds: Mine and yours:

Is the Earth for all of you, or just a few privileged families? Who decides who is privileged? What is a royal family? There is no hierarchy among humans. The modern world of human society and all previous and future societies, are nothing more than the manifestations of your imaginations – not actual realities. There are two worlds here on Earth running simultaneously. One is Me, Nature, or the natural-world, which you can disturb, destroy, adjust, impact, etc. But you did not construct Us and We have Our own rules and systems, and exist independently and in spite of your human existence, and most of you are unaware of how We work, despite being totally dependent on Us.

Then there is your world: the built environment, the exploitation of Our sources, your technology, etc. Which includes the illusory world of humans, the way each one of you views the world, the self-images you have within your structures, with all your emotions, yearning, desires, needs and wants; some necessary things, but just as many nonsensical. Fulfilling basic needs for all of you should be your guide: things like food, water, shelter, clothing,

(health care, security?)

The powerful among you, owners and shareholders of established large corporate interests, are preventing change to a new world, holding back the birth of new human systems, because you benefit so much from business as usual (BAU). However, BAU is now jeopardizing the ability of your own human survival and other life forms. Many tipping points are now approaching that could lead to various levels of disruption or unsustainability. In recent times, your corporate domination of institutions and governments has become the norm, never before seen.

In your lives you must now manifest, to the best of your abilities, the world needed to be a sustainable planet.

Don't you realize that everything that is good for Me, is also good for you, and vice versa?

During the recent Covid Pandemic, some of you somewhat awoke from the mesmerism of the pressures demanded by your modern world, based on the economy and Gross Domestic Product (GDP), instead of a world based on Life. Consequently, instead of being be-witched, some of you became de-witched!

The life and time you are born into is just a collective imagining. It can be constructed any way you wish. You could live in a sharing/caring world. Or/and a healthy/healing world. Ask yourselves, what kind of world would you like to live in? What kind of world would I like you to construct? Read on.

2. Universal Basic Income:

Imagine: Every person over 18 years old gets say, $1,000.00 US. a month tax free, whether working or not, in perpetuity. Is this shocking to you? One would hope that this would help secure people's basic needs, not wants or frivolous buying. Do I hear you saying people won't work and become lazy, etc.? Many have their objections to this, but it turns out, some of you have already experimented with this Universal Basic Income (UBI)?

The idea has been around since your antiquity, and in recent centuries has been considered in many forms including 'negative income tax' schemes. Now, there is great urgency with the maturation of full robot automation and the looming potential of AI, disrupting even non-physical careers. This brings up the question: Is the bounty of the world only owned by the super-rich? There are deep moral questions to consider, whether My sources may be regarded as 'the commons,' belonging to all. And going further, does 'all' include My non-human world of flora and fauna?

The transition to the needed new world of sustainability, deemed by Me as essential, let alone the loss of your jobs mentioned above, will mean you'll need this safety net. If justice and equity prevail in your new society, again, something akin to UBI will be necessary. There have been so many pilot projects around the world since the 1960s, anyone who wants to take a deep dive into the subject will find surprising results. It could lead to an increase in wellbeing, creativity and entrepreneurship, while reducing crime and drug abuse and hopefully more creative solutions on how to help Me.

Who will pay for this? Look at the tax codes. Since the 1980s, corporations and the ultra-rich have been writing their own tax percentages. When these taxes decrease the deficit increases, it may not be the direct result of government spending. What about the need for the public commons? Again, these lower taxes on corporations and the wealthy, hurt the funding of all public services. There is more than enough money to initiate UBI if the tax code becomes equitable. Would you like to live in a fair society? Those who have never lived paycheck to paycheck will probably not get this at all! If only you had my POV, (point of view) as they say in your Hollywood scripts!

3. Reduce Consumerism:

Here's where I kick you, big time, into the dilemma, and why the aforementioned UBI is necessary. You have to reduce your consumption by 50%. Ouch! See what I mean.

As a human society you have the responsibility to fulfill everyone's needs, (not necessarily wants), through what I see as a Basic Needs Economy, it would be unethical to behave otherwise. So, let's state some of these needs as a baseline for our exploration:

Nutritious Food and clean water (currently not predominant)

Adequate shelter in all seasons (No homelessness)

Adequate clothing for modesty and protection

Adequate healthcare from the healthcare industry, and lifestyle responsibility from you the people (not currently the case)

Sufficient income for the needs, not the 'wants'

Safe neighborhoods (a deliberate culture of caring)

Inclusion within a community or communities

Some communities succeeded in doing this in the past years of your history. However, far too many in the modern world are barely satisfying these needs. Of course, you have a capitalist society now, which means profit is the measure of everything. Well, you say, we have always been capitalists. No, not like today. "Currently, today's capitalism is the dominant economic paradigm, and private companies are amassing power. This tends to render socio-political relations between you humans invisible, for instance by making inequality seem natural, and by masking the indispensable role of government support that must come in to fill crucial gaps. In this context, it is important to differentiate between markets and capitalism. Your 20th century French thinker, Fernand Braudel, advances that 'the market' is characterized by common experience, openness, small profits, supply-and-demand determined pricing, controlled competition, involvement of ordinary people, and is a liberating force, whereas 'capitalism' is characterized by speculation, opacity, exceptional profit seeking, power determined pricing, elimination of competition, hegemonic power and monopoly-seeking. Capitalism is both anti-competitive and anti-market." (IPES report, Food From Somewhere, 2024)

I want to bring in the history of your 'stuff' production here to help inform our discussion. Since the 1920s, your years, you have been able to overproduce most basic goods with relative ease, including agricultural products. I think you should congratulate yourselves on this, not just the wealthy industrialists, but, the whole workforce that makes this happen. For the capitalist this is a dilemma, but for any animal species this is a relief.

"Ok, we've got it solved, let's have some leisure time and enjoy our family and relationships. I've always wanted to be creative and paint some landscapes, now I can. I've always wanted to read all the classics, now I can. This is the good-life and I'm not stressed anymore and in fact I feel healthier."

How come you don't have a life like this? It

should be possible for everyone. You've solved basic needs! What happened? Who or what drives the consumption monster? Is it your desire for stuff, or the super-wealthy owners/shareholders wanting more and more wealth?

Watch out here comes advertising, "but the thing I have is fine," you say. No, it's not, according to advertising. "But I can't afford all these things," then here comes credit. Then, you'll notice, that despite inventing amazing technology for over a hundred years, things break all the time. That is until 2015, when France became the first country in the world to make this new law: "Planned obsolescence means the techniques by which a manufacturer aims to deliberately reduce the life of a product to increase its replacement rate. It is punishable by two years of imprisonment and a fine of 300,000 Euros." It started with light bulbs in the US. Wow! Nowhere in the world was it illegal to make something that breaks deliberately. Do you know how difficult this immoral act is for Me? You now have a trinket economy as opposed to the one mentioned above, the basic needs economy.

Personal consumption expenditures are 70% of the US economy, a massive amount of non-essential items. Apart from the financial burden of this on you all, the social implications among you are debilitating. And I moan under this load: Resource extraction and depletion, waste disposal, resultant pollution, biodiversity loss, energy expended and emissions load, and on and on. This is why I must quote your Shakespeare here from Hamlet, with my modification: "Time is out of joint, oh, cursed spite, that you were born to set it right." Because you all delayed and continue to delay sufficient sustainability, your only position is to take extremely bold steps, despite altering the entire course of the world economy. It seems only the profiteers were watching the store, and with all you people being bombarded endlessly with messaging to buy, buy, buy, or you're worthless, the mass-mesmerism of the consumer economy won the day, despite being contrary to My planetary ecological boundaries. Now, for some of you, your very self-image is caught up in the ability, choice and act of consuming products – you are fallen ones.

Move from being be-witched, to de-witched. We have some people really assessing their place in the workforce. In China the students are 'lying flat' in protest of hyper-competition and in defense of rest and relaxation, similar to 'quiet quitting.' And 'letting it rot,' a way of expressing dejection and fatigue about the expectations around the ludicrous study and work schedules. The Chinese government has expressed displeasure around such protests, but I'm heartened to see that they are not living the life of automatons, but experiencing introspection that could even lead to wisdom and maybe sensible human existence.

A backlash to consumerism must become a movement for Me, and by extension your survival. The pushers of consumerism – celebrities, corporations, politicians, and the wealthy, etc., must cower to public pressure. "There will always be limits to growth. They can be self-imposed. If they aren't, they will be system-imposed." From one of your lights: Donella meadows, writing in her book, Thinking in Systems.

It's estimated that the U.S. lifestyle consumes the equivalent of 4 planets worth of resources. It's only because some of the world uses less than 1 planet's worth of resources that this is possible. As those nations lift themselves to a higher standard of living, the industrialized countries will ultimately have to reduce their consumption to prevent world-wide chaos; or not!

4. Make Planned Obsolescence Illegal:
You've got to help Me out here. Can you help make planned obsolescence illegal. I see coffee grinders being made with resisters in the wire to the motor, they have no purpose. There's a wire in, a switch and a motor. The resistor is put there to deliberately blow if the user pushes it a bit. The manufacturer would say, to protect the motor, but the size of the motor does not need protecting. This insidious practice, started it seems in modern times in the U.S. by a light bulb consortium in your 1920s. They reduced their bulbs from 2,500 hours of life to 1,000, and the money flowed in. You can bet that almost everything made today has a deliberate flaw built in. This is literally compromising Me by the material demand effects on my landscapes, energy used, resultant pollution, and by extension, contributing to your possible extinction.

Does that sound a bit extreme, it's not? The planet biosphere just can't keep supplying this level of resource extraction and subsequent waste load. Don't think the industrial countries are handling this, while the undeveloped world flunks when it mimics them. While writing this, a study showed that in the Philadelphia area, 15 billion gallons of raw sewage is released into the water-shed annually, rivers and streams, every year when heavy rains come and they can't handle the water treatment. You're kidding Me: 1.25 billion gallons a month? And that's just one city region, probably all the others are doing the same. The whole modern world is a shell game!

But, with social media, it will be easy to let folks know who the criminals are and who the built-to-last manufacturers are. With France being the first country to make planned obsolescence illegal, it's only a matter of time before everyone does, especially with your globalized supply chain. The computer industry, which flourishes on continual upgrades, must be a part of this and reform its gluttonous obsolescence appetite.

5. Make Right-To-Repair Mandatory:
Can you help make the 'right to repair' mandatory? Similar to built-in obsolescence, another deliberate ploy by manufacturers to make you buy more stuff with similar environmental repercussions. However, there is a new local small business economic development opportunity with this: Repair shops, does anyone remember those? Locally some are already doing this in the form of 'Repair Cafés.' Some people, on weekends, meet with toolboxes, sewing machines, soldering irons at the ready, and repair almost anything that comes through the door for free, at the amazement of those who bring their broken stuff.

Lots of you no longer know how to repair things, since the word 'engineer' now refers to someone involved in IT, not working with the analog world. The time has come when you've been raised in societies that don't repair. But there's hope: The Repair Café International Foundation has been trying to reverse this since 2011. Founded in the Netherlands, the movement has spread around the world.

It's certainly a generational thing. I remember your 1950s, it was unheard of not to repair something. Then as your time moved into the 1970s, I think, products were being produced in very low-income countries that for a person in an industrialized country to repair, was only a little less than buying a new one. So accelerated the throw-away-society. But by this time, we know that even if the consumer/citizen isn't the biggest direct loser, My environment is. Manufacturers now make products that are deliberately un-repairable. So, we are going to need you to vote for legislation to change this. Unless of course, through social media and product awareness, you will also pressure companies to change, once a critical mass of people realize this necessity. Probably a faster route than legislation, now I think of it.

6. Re-sue, Reduce, Recycle, Upcycle, Clean-up

Some of you know these things. In the book, Utopianism for a Dying Planet, the author writes: "We must reduce our desire for excessive consumption, or all the rest with be unachievable – indeed, is meaningless.

This does not mean renouncing the benefits of labor-saving devices like refrigerators, microwaves, vacuum cleaners, air conditioning, and central heating, or the amusements offered by radio, film, television, and the internet. It means, rather, using and adapting, and when required limiting, such devices, according to the criterion of sustainability." The 'criterion of sustainability,' I love this phrase, it must become one of your future guideposts in the sustain-age that you are very late initiating.

Re-use: Repair it and continue to use. Take the materials from a thing and re-use them to repair or make something else.

Reduce: Do you need that thing, really? Can you conserve in your daily rounds without really feeling deprived. E.g., use cold water instead of hot, this saves you magnitudes of energy, saves water and reduces pollution.

Recycle: You all know what this means, and in much of the world it's a lie. Very few things are actually recycled on an industrial scale. However, if you re-use, reduce, and upcycle, the need to recycle is unnecessary.

Upcycle: To upcycle you take a material that has been used before and with an effort less than would be needed to make a thing from original material, it is made into something useful. Downcycling is when you might crush, heat or completely reform a material for other use, often resulting in a lot more energy use, which We want to avoid.

Clean-up: Human-caused pollutants and waste in the world are at a staggering level and only likely to increase. In the book, Limits to Growth, they ran computer simulations of the major human factors affecting the world, this is on the list that could negatively impact human existence. That's why I put it in this section. You have to do clean-up way beyond a few super-fund sites, "the nation's worst hazardous waste sites." Everywhere has to be cleaned up, including the air you breath.

All this and more to save resources (My sources) and reduce the waste load on your societies. There's job reduction and creation here, with training in the new skills needed, and a major revolution in design. The threat to a circular economy, where raw materials can be used again and again, must be deflated by this rise in consciousness. A great re-skilling will be required – is your Youtube up to it? If you can keep the electricity on! (Oh, don't worry, AI will solve all this for you! Oh, I shouldn't snicker, aren't I awful, but I've been around a long time!)

7. Discourage Fashion In All Products:

This one's tough, but I want you to discourage fashion in all products. If ever there was a mass mesmerism among humans, I think fashion would be in the top ten. Look at your clothing, do you wear the mark of a slave? That swish, on the clothing, is the mark of a slave. Why you ask? Well, if you're a young person there's a lot of peer pressure that demands you have to wear the swish – does that sound like freedom? Their sneakers also have to be a certain brand, but there are perfectly good sneakers with no brand name, bought more cheaply from places like discount stores. But they're not allowed to wear these, so they are not free, but slaves to peer pressure and brand names.

Not just clothes, but cars, cell phones, etc. Again, this fashion leads to nonsensical over-production and waste/pollution because along with the above, the manufacturer can make you jettison your current products for the new version, even though they weren't worn out. Have mercy on Me! Either you stop this, or something in the future will stop it for you. That's not a threat, that's a built-in biosphere law.

8. Curtal Advertising:

Oh, boy, get this one: As a consequence of the 'authentic sustainability' efforts that you will be forced to adopt, this curtailment will happen, even if public pressure doesn't speed it up beforehand.

Imagine, if you can, traveling through the US in the year 1500 CE, before most of the European invaders (settlers) arrive. Apart from looking at virtually pristine landscapes wherever you went, there would be no advertising. No billboards and no phones, so no ads on the phone. You wouldn't be bombarded every second of the day with insidious advertising, someone trying to persuade you to buy their product, someone determined to mine your wallet and fill theirs. Advertising appears to be bent on destroying your peace, always trying to dissatisfy, pressure you. It's predatory. Say, "No, I am content."

I don't think you realize what this continual bombardment does to your psyches. I think it hijacks in you the fight or flight reaction, always right below the surface. Surely, it's a form of attack, a continual con.

If the Nature-reformed new world moves forward, an aware public will pressure ad agencies to reform.

I mentioned a de-witched state of mind earlier. This is where it's needed most. When enough people become de-witched by the illusions of their modern world, with all its fascinating technologies and special effects, and realize that every human world is just the projection of someone's imagination, they can ask themselves, what kind of future world do I want to live in?

It doesn't have to be dystopian. Although most people's minds go to this when asked about the future. My billboard would read: "Welcome to the future you had trouble imagining, because you were veiled by the strength of what you thought was reality. Fortunately, others among you have been working on something they think you'll come to love. It's about you and your love of family, friends and community. And about you being in charge of your time, with the ability to use most of it how you choose."

9. Revamp Financial System:

What's the thing that has failed you and caused upheaval many times already? Your ridiculous financial system.

This is being forced to change as I write this. Unrestrained capitalism appears to have reached its limit, maybe as early as 2008, at the beginning of the Great Recession. It has been propped up in several ways ever since. Those who make the most from the 'old' system will fight tooth, are fighting tooth and nail to keep their pet dinosaurs alive, preventing the new world from birthing.

By preventing the new world from birthing, by putting off what should be natural transitions, they will usher in chaos, frantic collapse and panic scenarios. And they will blame 'flaming Nature lovers' like me for causing it, when in fact their draconian attitudes and refusal to evolve caused it. This is the refusal to accept feedback from the systems and then self-regulate, a Permaculture Principle, well known to lifelong learners. I, Nature, do this automatically and so are always adjusting, I can't choose, like humans in a system, and be stubborn!

Growth is essential for capitalism, but it's fatal for Our planet. Because the planet is a finite biological and botanical world that is interconnected and interdependent, the whole system is self-correcting. If you insist on a growth imperative, don't expect your grandchildren to bless you in your grave.

The Degrowth imperative leads to what's being called a 'steady-state' economy. Finally, there are a lot of your experts studying this subject. At the World Economic Forum website it says, "The idea is that by pursuing degrowth policies, economies can help themselves, their citizens and the planet by becoming more sustainable."

In recent years, the financial system, above all other systems, has been the most volatile. So, no one can really argue that its form is the best humans can hope for. We saw in the debacle of the financial institutions of 2008, how they immediately embraced socialization for their losses and privatization for profits. It was such a blatant show. The so-called free market fell apart and public money had to pour in to save it. During the Plague of the early 2020s we saw some similar fancy footwork. Changes that were deemed impossible occurred overnight.

It's a complex sprawling field to work in. But, from the world I'm presenting here, we can all see that the financial system will have to flex, bend, and kicking and screaming, fundamentally evolve to serve the new world of sustainability. This is natural – natural being something not often allowed to happen in human constructed systems. Perhaps some economist, with an open mind, could take this on and write a book about it, showing you all what it might look like, a kind of future financial birthing manual. Perhaps, Kate Raworth has already given it in Doughnut Economics, where she says an economy should be designed to thrive, not grow.

10. Subsidize Income For: Farm Workers (farmers), School Teachers, Police, Healthcare Workers, Social Workers:

This is on top of UBI. Society found out how essential these workers were during the Plague of the early 2020s. These occupations were needed every day, sometimes 3 times a day, like farm workers. So, it's time to get some equity into the wage structure and stop allowing the influential people to write their own paychecks.

Some might think, well that's how it is, some people get paid well and others don't. But this is all a construct, which means it can be otherwise. The wealthy lady doesn't want to pay the help too high a wage, as she might have to do the cleaning herself.

Of course, many farm workers are in the construct of Agribusiness, large corporations with shareholders who don't want to see their wealth reduced. Even many of the so-called family farmers are now beholding to a mega-corporation, just sub-contractors told what to grow and how to grow it. With a predetermined action plan of buying GMO seed, fertilizer, pesticide, herbicide, fancy machinery to make all this happen, fancy loans to be able to purchase all this, and price setting by the market or corporation.

No wonder suicide is so high among farmers, it is three and a half times higher than among the general population, according to the National Rural Health Association.

The high-tech IT geniuses and others found out during the Plague that their luck and ability to work from anywhere was partly dependent on the school system being able to take their children. It showed the importance of school teachers, long-time underpaid with unrelenting daily schedules. What makes the lawyer worth so much more than the farmer? Probably the lawyer! I know there are large education debts to pay back and years of study, but what about a farmer with 30-years-experience and study, what's that worth when it's putting the food on the lawyer's table 3 times a day?

There is so much out of joint, time to put it right. You're not looking at your own human society as an ecology, which is what it is. How can I expect you to take care of Me, when you don't take care of your own?

11. De-commodify Food, Education, Healthcare

"Like the other great revolutions, (agriculture and industrial), the coming sustainability revolution will also change the face of the land and the foundations of human identities, institutions and cultures." (Book: Limits to Growth, The 30-year Update).

If you de-commodify food, education and healthcare, "The relation that individuals and communities maintain with these goods and services is changed, decision-making processes are redefined, and governance re-shaped." (From: De-commodification as a foundation for ecological economics, https://sciencedirect.com)

Foundation for ecological economics, I like that! These three are not desire-products and decoupling them from the market would surely help stabilize their availability and price. Do we want to make profit from someone's illness? Is it not on the immoral side to pay shareholder dividends on these, especially, in many cases, because they are often subsidized up front by citizen's taxes? Why should corporations make profits from your subsidies? Ans: Because business is business, and leads to getting money anyway possible, legitimately or in a 'legally' fraudulent manner in today's market. These things affect My biosphere which ultimately affects your ability to thrive.

According to, A Long Food Movement: Transforming Food Systems by 2045, IPES, International Panel of Experts on Sustainable Food Systems: "...the locus of power in food systems and the broader global economy is shifting at dizzying speed. In 2008, the world's most powerful corporations drilled oil wells and traded stocks. Twelve years later, the world's five corporate titans all deal in intangible data and have a market valuation that exceeds the GDP of entire continents. 'Multi-stakeholderism' is everywhere as corporations – sensing the social and environmental tipping points ahead – seek to draw governments, scientists and a handful of civil society organizations into an artificial new multilateralism....(one future scenario could be:) putting food security at the mercy of digital networks and potential data glitches would worry governments and (the) food movement alike...With food seen as a strategic asset, a new wave of land, ocean, and resource grabs could get underway, and trade chokepoints (become) increasingly militarized."

Your private sector, it seems to Me, detests publicly run or state-run entities. They tell you they are inefficient and that they could do it better – but history shows this is nothing but a money grab. And education tax dollars appear to be in the throes of that today.

However, clearly the volatility of the coming years, if not the present, will crash certain models and raise up new ones in the debris of past institutions. Public education appears to be in these throes right now, where will it land? Hopefully, not privatized, where shareholders take their profit and decide what your children learn, but also in a better place than it is now. I'll tell you how I want education to be in a minute. As for healthcare, I see your hospitals closing all over. Your population appears extremely sick from the consumption of ultra-processed foods and between that and the accountants running the hospitals, not health care professionals, these systems appear to be headed for collapse in the not-too-distant future. Then no private company will come near it – until it is profitable once again.

12. Re-localize the Food System Worldwide (Encourage locally sourced lifestyles)

What is a local food system? "Local and regional food systems" refers to place-specific clusters of agricultural producers of all kinds – farmers, ranchers, fishers – along with consumers and institutions engaged in producing, processing, distributing, and selling foods. (USDA report). You've got to do this for Me and you.

Shouldn't food be everywhere? By re-localizing the food system worldwide, food is everywhere and will not need to be shipped from thousands of miles away, reliant on other lands, as it is now. This will surely encourage every country to treasure their arable lands and water systems while appreciating where their food originates. What's good for you is good for Me!

Many of your city regions only grow about 6% of their food, does that sound like food security to anyone? You're not even looking out for yourselves. Please! I mean you want economic activity, it's all some of you live for. These area food systems are multi-billion-dollar businesses and includes: transport, refrigeration, growing and processing, restaurants, beverages, accounting, law, contracts, machinery, tools, etc., and many other things like training, culinary, land and real estate business. It follows that food security would be enhanced, facilitates economic development, job creation, community building, food growing knowledge increased locally, and possibly a health improver.

This would help Us both with climate change impacts, fossil fuel reduction, increased sustainability, soil and land preservation, may improve worldwide water quality and availability, reduces carbon footprint, may help increase social justice, reduce

By Tony Buck — A catalyst for economic development?

deforestation and make regions more resilient. It may also facilitate more 'direct to consumer' (DTC) sales, which currently increase year after year, compensating farmers better and getting more nutritious product to citizens. Of course, this would need to be established in an organic, regenerative agriculture system, unlike your current agricide model. I got more to say on that. There was a report called, Trends in U.S. Local and Regional Food Systems: A Report to Congress, AP -068, Economic Research Service/USDA, so if the government has noticed a trend, we can surmise that this is already moving, all be it, slowly.

Also, according to Dr. Alexander Muller of TEEBAgFood and its research initiatives, "Agriculture is arguably the highest policy priority on today's global political agenda, in recognition of its widespread impacts on food security, employment, climate change, human health, and severe environmental degradation (yikes you're telling Me!)…Food is one of the most important and pressing issues for sustainability and human wellbeing. It has major positive or (unfortunately very often) negative impacts on natural resources, it shapes the landscape worldwide, it generates income for billions of people, and it is linked with knowledge, education, social equity, and global justice. If we do not transform today's agriculture into real sustainable food systems, we will not achieve the U.N. Sustainable Development Goals (SDGs)…"

Threats to food security from the worldwide food supply chain includes: Climate change/weather - disruption - drought, long-distance transport disruption, rising costs of transport fuels and their carbon footprint, soil depletion from bad practices, deforestation, local conflict, civil rights abuses throughout the supply chain, including land grabs. So, in a world moving from 8 billion to 10 billion people, trying to build a more caring society, this is surely a high priority towards a more sustainable, resilient, life-support system.

Encouraging locally sourced lifestyles for everything, goes along with this. With more time and universal basic income, (UBI), I'm sure there will be a flourishing of what I'm calling *Hentrepreneurs*: Household economy entrepreneurs. People making crafts, products and small businesses from locally sourced raw materials. With your new consciousness, searching for locally made products, before ordering them from far-off, will become second nature, I hope.

13. Reduce Agricide, Increase Regenerative Agriculture Worldwide:

Ok, now you got me started. Many of you won't understand this without some back-story, being so disconnected from your food system these days. So here goes.

In the early twentieth century the chemical Haber/Bosch process led to the ability to make nitrogen fertilizer, whereas agriculture until that time relied on natural substances like animal manure or guano from sea birds. This process relies heavily on fossil fuels for its production.

After the second-world-war, the chemical industry involvement in agriculture increased exponentially. It helped fuel what is called the 'green revolution.' This agriculture, heavily dependent on fossil fuel chemical production for fertilizer, pesticides and herbicides, expensive machinery, land acquisition (larger areas farmed), genetic modification of seeds, did indeed increase food and feed output tremendously, but at what cost?

So, this modern agriculture sends chemical runoffs into streams and oceans causing dead zones, (currently 415 worldwide, National Geographic Society), monocultures leading to super bugs and increased plant disease, massive biodiversity loss, deforestation, large carbon footprint, soil erosion, etc., make these practices not only damaging now, but worse as time goes on and eventually unsustainable, as non-renewable fossil fuels deplete into the future. Within the industrial animal production side of agriculture, similar problems exist, including the vast inhumane aspect of the system, and the outsized inefficiency of turning plant foods into meat. (More in: Encourage Plant Based Eating).

This has led to what some call the Agribusiness/pharmaceutical complex. Some companies own and supply the seed, the chemical processes and pharmaceutical products. Many of the human intended 'foods' produced by this system, some call them 'feed' not food, also include ultra-processed foods that many now rely heavily on for their nutrition and that are not nutritious enough to support human health, and are in fact engineered to be addictive. Many current illnesses you have (80% Cleveland Clinic), are what are called 'lifestyle' diseases and can be directly linked to diets heavily dependent on ultra-processed foods.

Although many people around the world are dependent on this system, in 2022, more than 700 million people faced hunger and 2.4 billion people lacked year-round access to sufficient and nutritious food, according to the United Nations – therefore it hasn't alleviated hunger.

That's why many people consider this form of agriculture unsustainable and call for what is variously called, regenerative farming practices, restoration agriculture, agroforestry, organic agriculture, etc., to restore soil health, reduce pollution, reverse biodiversity loss, use less water, benefiting both communities and planet. (Yeah!) These practices would probably benefit from smaller farms, individually owned and locally distributed everywhere. Critics to this say, "we can't feed the world this way," but remember, throw away your idea of today's farm being owned and worked by a farm family producing a large variety of products in an idyllic countryside setting. From my vantage point I can see all this, for many of you this is far off and hidden.

In the future you might seek guidance from the design practice of Permaculture, which is based in careful observation, gathering information and experiences to promote understanding of Nature, the landscape and the people involved. Thus, Permaculture food systems are information and design intensive, whereas traditional agriculture was labor intensive, and industrial agriculture is energy intensive (Holmgren, 2002). This applies at all scales from the garden to the farm.

This is such an immense subject, that I'll let Mark Hyman, MD, author of Food Fix conclude this section:

"There is one place that nearly everything that matters in the world today converges: our food and our food system – the complex web of how we grow food, how we produce, distribute, and promote it; what we eat, what we waste, and the policies that perpetuate unimaginable suffering and destruction across the globe that deplete our human, social, economic, and natural capital...Food is the nexus of most of the world's health, economic, environmental, climate, social, and even political crises. While this may seem like an exaggeration, it is not. The problem is much worse than we think." And some of you are worried about peak oil, you should also consider peak soil. It takes Me 800 years to make 1 inch of soil from rocks, while billions of tons washes into the ocean and/or is destroyed every year by your mismanagement. Be humbled, without soil you do not exist.

14.   Reduce Animal Food Consumption World-wide:

You might think that the Plague of the early 2020s (Pandemic) was a health-crisis, and indeed that is what it became. But actually, it started within your now 'indefinite' world-wide food crisis for the foreseeable future. That's if you accept that being a zoonotic disease, COVID, came from a pangolin, or some such wild animal, within the Chinese wild animal economy, which amounts to billions in sales annually, far from being a fringe operation. After all they've got to find about 4 billion meals a day to feed their people.

Part of the way to address the food crises is to reduce animal-food consumption. In fact, going forward it is an imperative. That's why, when I saw a 26 floor, high-rise pig farm in China, my jaw just dropped. Approximately 600,000 pigs in one building, as much as one million pounds of feed going in a day, then how much waste per day coming out? What to do with it? This seems to me to be the height of ignorance. Maybe just an animal industry having its way, I know they're feeding almost 4 times the US population, but clearly, they haven't thought through what a smart diet would be?

The knowledge has been out there for a long time (in your terms). In the foreword to John Robbins' book, Diet for a New America, 1987, Joanna Macy imagines a world that adopted some of the information he documented there: "We find that the grain we previously fed to fatten livestock can now feed five times the U.S. population;...The great forests of the world, that we had been decimating for grazing purposes (that was, we discover, the major cause of deforestation), begin to grow again...As we stop raising and grinding up cattle for hamburgers, we discover that ranching and farm factories had been the major drain on our water resources."

With over a billion people to feed a day, you'd think feeding the grain, or spending that money to buy a plant product that can be turned into protein, like soy beans, or any other bean, would help solve so many of the Chinese food system's problems, even as crop disruption from climate change decreases yields!

U.S. meat consumption is three times the global average, this is not only unhealthy, it is unnecessary. It is also a choice. Melanie Joy, PhD, Edm, wrote the book, Why We Love Dogs, Eat Pigs, and Wear Cows. She also started the website, Beyond Carnism. She says, "Carnism is the invisible belief system, or ideology, that conditions people to eat certain animals." Also, "Most people are opposed to such violence, (the raising and slaughtering of animals for their consumption), and so to keep itself intact, carnism uses a set of psychological defense mechanisms designed to prevent people from becoming aware of the violence of the system or of the fact that the system even exists."

Another reason: "the same antibiotics that humans need, are used for animal health. In fact, the (antibiotic) overuse in animal agriculture is now considered a global health threat because it could lead to antimicrobial resistance. 80% of antibiotics sold in the United States are for animal agriculture and expected to increase worldwide as time continues. The practice of medicine and the state of public health would be catastrophically affected if antibiotics were not generally effective in treating bacterial illnesses.
(www.ncbi.nim.nih.gov/pmc/articles/PMC4638249/)

It seems to Me that there will be no choice to reduce animal consumption in the future for a sustainable planet. The tens of billions of animals incarcerated in this system complain to a Higher Power every day, if their prayers ever get fulfilled, the human carnivores will hear about it.

15. Encourage Plant-based Eating

So, continuing, let's encourage plant-based eating. I have already touched on some of it, but let's make it easy at a glance:

More sustainable with population growth, climate impacts, resource and water depletion

Healthier lifestyle

Reduce the chance of zoonotic disease outbreaks from the edible wild animals and domestic animal market

Cheaper

Reduces deforestation

Cuts fossil fuel use

Plants are less complex to produce than animals

Opportunities for innovation (indoor vertical farms, urban rooftop mini-farms, etc.)

Opportunity for households to provision themselves for more self-reliance

With re-localization of food system, many opportunities for food innovators and processors, local businesses

Safer food supply

More compostable waste stream (even at the household level)

Less animal waste and the huge negative ecological impacts associated with that

Less negative impact on the antibiotic supply.   Less methane gas production

16.   Re-skill For Home Cooking, Reduce Processed Food Intake:

I keep hearing humans say, they have no time to cook. And yet according to the numbers, people watch at least four hours of some kind of media every day. Here's the amazing thing, you can continue watching media while you cook! This goes along with the reduction of agricide and the industrial highly processed food system. And the fact that doctors, who are mainly nutritionally illiterate, will, I think, focus more on this when the health system breaks from the sickness generated by the old system.

Now when you have a 50% reduction in consumerism, a shorter workweek, universal basic income, everyone will have more time to cook. I'm distinguishing cooking with whole recognizable foods, from heating up pre-packaged, sugar-weighted, processed edible substances made by corporations.

There's a lot of people watching cooking shows at home, and the kids are primed ready for it. To Me, cooking yourself a great quality meal is one of the best gifts you can give yourself. You should never have let this go. Relocalizing the food system is sure to encourage this, what a renaissance that could lead to.

Of course, it should be concentrated on heavily plant-based ingredients for a sustainable world.

And that would naturally lead to encouraging an organic edible gardening lifestyle, totally feeding into the re-localized food system. Your ancestor's Victory Garden effort of the second-world-war was said to have supplied as much as 40% of vegetable produce for those involved. And I'm sure it increased appreciation for food growing that you sadly lack today. (This disconnection among you is at an all-time high, and may be why modern society tolerates such high land pollution levels.) This gardening lifestyle, helps keep vital knowledge within the citizenry, and with the introduction of self-reliant education, becomes a lifestyle practice. You can cancel that subscription to the gym!

"Responding to climate change will entail massive socio-emotional and behavioral changes." (Recent National Academies workshop document). In that vein I offer this quote: "digging in a garden" was one of the activities that distinguished those male patients who recovered from their mania from those that did not.' Nothing has changed in this field since then. (From Dr. Benjamin Rush 1812, Medical Inquiries and Observations Upon Diseases of the Mind, page 226, professor of the Institute of Medicine and Clinical Practice at the University of Pennsylvania, and known for his role in the development of modern psychiatry.)

One hallmark of self-reliant education will be outdoor classrooms in public schools where contact with Nature reinforces this activity. This compliments home cooking and provisioning, while having mental and physical health benefits for all. Living with organic gardens will naturally put pressure on the current agricide food production model, and one would hope with the whole citizenry engaged in this, invention and best practices will flourish and be shared worldwide through word and mouth and electronic media. About two in five American households now practice some food growing in their gardens, approximately 50 plus million homes. It's not hard to see that this concept for a livable future is probably the most advanced. No garden, no problem. There are initiatives called 'garden share,' where those with excess garden or physically unable to work their garden, share with others, (there's an app for that), and of course, community gardens and/or allotments in most regions.

It's very hard to grow all your own food, especially proteins. You can certainly grow the majority of specialized vegetables like greens, salads, herbs, and fruits, which contain the real specific nutrients like vitamins, phytochemicals, minerals and micro-nutrients. And with a warming planet, growing through winters will be even easier. Saving money while getting exercise! Also, take into account all the unnecessary trips to the store by vehicle. All going in the right direction for Me and you.

17. Revamp Public Education:

Please revamp all your education efforts. Completely! The children will thank you and I will thank you, and the whole society will be thankful. I thought your schooling had become more relevant in recent years, but I hear young students talking among themselves that they are still taught that fascist, unjust, merciless civilizations, like the Egyptians, are 'great' civilizations. So, a child might ask, "If I go home and force my neighbors to pile up all the rocks in my garden into the shape of a pyramid, will I be great?"

Some children are still taught that the history of the royal families of their countries is their history. What, the history of the most murderous, oppressive people in the land is their history? Where is the history of the people's families? How will you teach the history of this time if My tipping points start going off? What education will the society need then?

Your public-school education appears to be in a heightened crisis since the end of the Plague of the early 2020s (Pandemic): Charter schools gutting the public-school tbudgets, teachers leaving on mass having awoken to their predicament, culture attacks coming from many quarters, under-funded institutions, etc. Large dropout and truant numbers in schools. Youth unemployment in China has skyrocketed with so many graduates. Where does all this end up? Will we see radical changes in the near future?

The late Sir Ken Robinson, educator, says there's a revolution underway tied to technology and population growth, consequences as yet unknown. Again, something localized may be in the model change, not federally mandated, leaving so many kids behind. Even college futures are unpredictable right now with students questioning the return on such high costs.

It's interesting that Ken Robinson equates the current education system to industrialized agriculture, touted by some as a success, without acknowledging the huge problems it's caused and that it's unsustainable. He says our social systems suffer from the same problems. It's time to reinvent.

What if the focus of your education system helps you live in your immediate environment? Something to do with understanding the houses you live in, landscapes, utilities, built environment, neighborhoods, waste water, the effects of climate change, and less corporation dependent family provisioning, less dependent on worldwide supply chains, educating for a true sense of place and your interactions with it. What would that look like?

18. 5 – 12 Years Old, Self-reliant, Systems Thinking Education:

My proposal for 5 – 12 years old, self-reliant, systems thinking education.

You used to say don't give a person fish, teach that person to fish. That is no longer applicable, now you need to teach that person about the system the fish swims in. I see people fishing above a steel mill thinking the fish are healthier there with less pollution. But because they don't understand the system around them, they don't know that the steel mill doesn't dump water into the river any more. However, the biggest polluter is all around them nevertheless: runoff from industrialized agriculture (agricide): fertilizer, pesticide and herbicides all toxic to the creatures in My biosphere.

"System: A set of elements or parts that is coherently organized and interconnected in a pattern or structure that produces a characteristic set of behaviors, often classified as its 'function" or "purpose.""" (Donella H. Meadows, Thinking in Systems, 2008)

Example: The fire that destroyed the town of Lahaina, on the island of Maui, in 2023, wasn't responsible for the destruction, the system that surrounded it was. Public works, landscaping (invasive grasses growing everywhere), codes department, town management, fire department, dysfunctional water resources, utility supplier, etc., the interconnected, interdependent elements of the built and My Natural environment. If you think only fire, you might issue fire extinguishers to the next residents, and that wouldn't be of any use to prevent a similar situation.

You can teach this to your children. It's a more accurate view of planet Earth. Why aren't you teaching this to every student at college level? Can you imagine the creative thinking skills the children would acquire through this and how that would feed into their understanding of the world? Good for Me, good for your futures. Of course, what I'm suggesting here would also require the re-education of teachers.

Other teaching styles like project-based learning, and putting the A for arts into the STEM curriculum, while emphasizing life-long learning, should be explored. And outdoor classroom spaces should be built into all school property designs and used. Last Child in the Woods author, Richard Louv, is pioneering more Nature education due to his concept of Nature Deficit Disorder, maintaining that the children benefit so much from this, as I would.

I think all this and more, a self-reliant component would produce engaged, dynamic students. Add to their activities: cooking, carpentry, metal work, tool use, repair skills, house care, gardening; within a nature setting, all the collecting, observation, foraging, explanation of natural systems right in their backyard, flora and fauna, knowledge of place; all the curriculum standards would be incorporated within this structure, math, language, etc., exposure to them would flow naturally from their interactions and need to measure and document; as blackboards fade into the background. Imagine a child telling the mother, "No need to call the plumber, I'll fix the flushing system in the toilet tank!" From 5 to 12 years old, confident of their place in their world, knowing their world, loving their world.

"The future of our planet depends on a change of consciousness, in which the people and the resources of the natural world are no longer taken for granted and exploited without considering long term impacts. Supporting children from early childhood to develop a sensitive, compassionate and cooperative relationship with each other and the natural world is a crucial step in generating this new consciousness." See, some of you know: Earth Care, People Care, And Fair Share in Education: The Children in Permaculture Manual, 2018.

It seems to me that current elementary, middle and high school education doesn't teach self-reliance, but prepares people for dependency on corporations; even your degree turns you into beggars, having to hawk the degree around to beg for a job!

12 – 18 years old, corporate education, what exists today, I'll hand this back to you. Pick it up at grade 8. Children exposed to My self-reliant education may have something to say about the style of this continuation toward the college years.

19. Champion All Renewable Energy, NOT Nuclear:

Amory Lovins, co-founder of the Rocky Mountain Institute : "We don't need any novel technology we need smarter design."

Despite everything, the adoption of renewables is becoming normalized. You're still a long way off because the electric grid also needs to be upgraded and segmented, networked and improved mightily to handle the new world of renewable electricity.

It is understood that the amount of energy from oil is so unbelievable that it will be hard for renewables to deliver that level of output. But, many of your systems are also unbelievably inefficient – a result of cheap energy in the past. It is time to focus not on new invention, but to put all your attention on negawatts, the ones you don't use. Simply, if you insulated more fully all the buildings in every country, you probably wouldn't need to build any more power generating stations for some time, especially in the industrialized countries. And with transport switching to electric power, you're going to need as much as you can get. I've only mentioned the built environment, but there are so many other places energy can be conserved, so let's get with this.

Wind and solar seem to be the big go-toes right now. Geothermal, using the heat/cooling advantage from under the surface of the earth is another. But you only go shallow for this at the moment. Recently, people have been talking about the vast amount of energy deeper in the earth, it's a no-brainer for you to tap that and the oil industry is going to help you. Why? Because the drilling and fracking technologies they've developed are just what you need to go down great depths for much higher temperatures. Future towns could be heated just from this system alone from a centralized distribution center. This is already in use in countries where they have natural geothermal features near the Earth's surface.

Note from me: Below the planet's surface, what you call the frost-line in the earth, the depth at which the earth freezes in winter, it's a constant 45-50 degrees, this is normal the world over where there isn't permafrost and even in very hot countries. What are the connotations of this? If buildings have a below-surface floor, known currently as a basement or cellar, and if future buildings are dug a little deeper, here you have a cool place to live in the possible super-hot climate of the future, without the need of any extra cooling energy. In fact, you might need a small intake fan to bring the warm air from outside, just to bring the temperature up a little to be more comfortable. Look to Us (Nature) for solutions first before making a big hoo-ha industry out of it – not your modern way.

Nuclear power is not zero emissions. Radioactive material is mined in far-off countries, sometimes under very insecure conditions. Then shipped to a processing destination. This highly toxic material has special handling needs. Then the power station is built with lots of concrete and steel, which uses and gives off emissions for decades. No one will insure them, so the people have to, through government agreements and that should tell you something. Huge amounts of water are consumed, putting a strain on local habitat. Then, when decommissioned, the infrastructure has to be maintained for 50,000 years. And the waste has to be stored... somewhere, for thousands of years. Should you put this burden on future people who didn't benefit from its short life span? And all the while there is always the possibility of a major accident, the consequences of that make it so irresponsible. Take a look at Fukushima, Japan. You seriously contaminated all My ecology for miles around. If a wind turbine falls, you collect the pieces, recycle what you can and replace it; if nuclear power stations fail, they could destroy Me, Nature itself, (which, do I need to remind you, is you also), it should never be on the surface of the planet. It's time to give Me a position on the board of every corporation in the world, with voting rights just like the other participants!

20. Continue To Reduce Fossil Fuel Use:

This is the time the fossil fuel/oil industry has dreaded for the last 50 years of their mischievous existence. They have marketed, lied and cheated to retain their polluting product's dominance – the reckoning is nigh! And it is time to pay the real price for the product, no more externals, (outsourcing side-effect costs to other sectors of the economy).

"Air pollution from transportation sources caused an estimated 74,00 deaths in India in 2015, out of which two-thirds, (66%) could be attributed to tailpipe emissions from diesel vehicles on the road," according to estimates in the global report by researchers from the International Council on Clean Transportation (CCT), George Washington University, and University of Colorado Boulder. And, of course, the burning of fossil fuels has caused such high concentrations of carbon dioxide in the atmosphere that it's leading to what most scientist consider catastrophic climate change.

In, Unlocking Sustainable Cities by Paul Chatterton, 2019, it informs us: "Moreover, the sheer amount of public subsidies that go into maintaining car culture is staggering... (Which translates to, we are subsidizing climate change!) Car culture therefore, is one of the key drivers pushing the finite global biosphere towards its limits...Unlocking alternative transport futures can only go hand in hand with a shift in planning and zoning, eroding the need for mass, wasteful commuting from neighborhood to work zones. Central areas need to be dispersed, work needs to be more broadly distributed, and food, leisure and retail needs rescaling and decoupling from car use. Starting with the car may seem parochial, but it points to the multiple steps unlocking real change for sustainable cities."

See, unbelievable, this knowledge is extent. Can you imagine life without the car? Go on try. What would it look like? Lots of redesign of everything, you'll need to go deep, and, deeper still. It's only about 100 years that this infernal combustion engine has been around. Your (and My) existence, now, literally depends on ending its reign. 40% of city space is dedicated to the car and they sit idle 95% of the time!

Al Gore quote: "They (fossil fuel industry) have used fraud and falsehoods on an industrial scale. And by lavishly funding their legacy networks of political and economic power, they have captured the policymaking process in too many countries around the world."

The misinformation campaigns of the fossil fuel industry are heavily financed to the tune of tens of millions of dollars a year. Imagine that, no wonder you are where you are, 50 years behind the (your) times by my reckoning. Does this reach the criteria of evil, or just immoral? When my self-reliant educated children reach sufficient numbers, watch out.

21. Conserve Energy, Insulate, Smart Design, etc.

I've already touched on this a little in, champion renewable energy, but what else is there?

With self-reliant education, the ability to innovate becomes widespread, leading to better solutions and design. Knowledge of systems leads to better resource use, conservation, including the all-important water infrastructure. Sustainability is now the thread running through all industry and people.

What if your neighborhoods were so well re-designed, with citizen participation and revivified community involvement, that you didn't feel the need to leave them, or even go for a Sunday drive? Mass movement of people by cars or other means must be reduced. What are the design implications of this? We're going to need designers: architects, city planners, engineers, pushing those pencils, oh, I mean, computer-design applications. Also recognizing, that this new opportunity is going to affect your grandchildren's ability to enjoy a thriving life. To reach the necessary new world, you're going to be very busy, and short term, may have to increase consumption and energy use a little, what an irony! But I get that.

22. Empower Women World-wide:

Through online education: skills, culture, websites, languages, natal care, nutrition education, small farming apps, water management, etc., mainly for women, especially in the southern hemisphere, if they can be supplied with cell phones with internet access, there has never been such an opportunity to improve their social foundation. I think it's understood that women's closeness to the children, makes them more responsible than males. If they could gain better access to birth control, biological knowledge, science-based self-care, complementing folk and herbal systems, I'm sure their overall health and the health of children would improve exponentially, also reducing child mortality.

Globally, women account for approximately 43% of the agricultural labor, in some countries that figure goes to 70%. Also, according to research from the U.N. Food and Ag Organization, if women farmers had the same access to resources as men, (including finance) the number of hungry people worldwide could be reduced by 150 million. And increasing their environmental knowledge and the consequences of their society's behavior, could only be a boon to Us.

According to Project Drawdown: "One outcome of family planning and education, slower global population growth, can contribute to reduced carbon emissions over time…Global population levels are a key variable in climate models, including those used by Intergovernmental Panel on Climate Change.

Unsustainable levels of consumption in high-income countries remain the primary driver of climate change, many of Project Drawdown's solutions focus on transforming the electricity, building, and energy sectors to drastically reduce emissions. People living in low-and middle-income countries are first and worst impacted by climate change. Fostering equality through family planning and universal education are vital components to attain higher levels of economic growth and sustained improvements in human well-being."

23. Innovate Less Harmful Air Conditioning Systems:

You've got to innovate less harmful air conditioning systems. You lot heated up the world, now you want to be cool so, no more industry snow-jobs. Adopt as many smart heat-reducing natural systems design as possible: Overhangs on buildings, reflective roofs, below ground living, etc. Use My Nature's systems as helpers: tree cover creating shade. Can you adopt safari roofs (double roofs, separated by a space) in your designs? Do solar panels on roof reduce heat build-up in attic? Understand the passive and the mechanical. There are many below ground solutions that need to be researched. Project Drawdown's Alternative Refrigerants solution consists of the gradual replacement of hydrofluorocarbon (HFCs), which are highly potent greenhouse gases, by alternative refrigerants, including ammonia, carbon dioxide, propane, and isobutene. Refrigerants are used in commercial refrigeration systems: in household appliances such as air conditioners and refrigerators; in refrigerated containers used for carrying perishable goods; as air conditioning systems on board cars, trains, aircrafts, and ships: in industrial cooling systems; and more.

The impact of improving these systems is one of the greatest single things you can do to help prevent further climate destruction. The profit motive prevents many companies from doing the best thing for the climate, so further legislation may be required. I know they'll scream about this, but believe it or not, the planet and Our convivial survival is more important than their short-term profits.

24. Encourage Faith Communities To Get Involved:

Become stewards of the Earth and less of the 'dominion over all' mentality. Think about it, the 'so-called' Christian nations have harmed the Earth more than any other people. They even created boarding schools in the U.S. and Canada to ruthlessly beat the Nature spirituality out of Native Americans (Turtle Island Natives). Can/will all faith communities be magnanimous enough to now join all other moderns in the new lifestyle necessary to avert the degradation of the planet, so that it can continue to support human and non-human life?

"Individualism and shortsightedness are the greatest problems of the current social system, we think (the authors), and the deepest cause of un-sustainability. Love and compassion institutionalized in collective solutions is the better alternative…The sustainability revolution will have to be, above all, a collective transformation that permits the best of human nature, rather than the worst, to be expressed and nurtured." (From, Limits to Growth: The thirty-year update, 2004).

"I'll be the first to say that the religious

environmental movement has been late in forming. Despite the prescient wisdom of some who came before, like St. Francis and before him St. Augustine, we haven't had much time to compare notes or agree on a global strategy for interfaith action. This new call to put faith into action is only a few years old….

Gradually, work of Interfaith Power and Light (IPL) spread and was picked up in the media, causing a large charitable foundation to seek us out and offer to help us hire a national campaign manager and take our

California model into other states… Thomas Berry, a well-known theologian and social historian… asks, "Is the human race sustainable?" I think the answer is, yes, but… We will need to become conscious of our behavior, follow faith's call to be stewards of Creation and believe in the power of the Spirit to move us toward a healthy planet. The goal is simple, the means are going to involve us all." (Rev. Canon Sally Bingham, Love God, Heal Earth, 2009)

Christian monotheism may not appear to address the preservation of Me, (Nature) specifically with instructions like, "shall have dominion over the Earth," and other such phrases, but it is implicit in the prayer, "Thy will be done." Therefore, it is incumbent upon the Judeo/Christian/Islamic people to acknowledge the will of God in Nature. And what is that? Let's explore from the empirical evidence.

There is 'succession,' the tendency for all land to go through stages from bare ground to rain-forest.

You'll have noticed that your garden has a will of its own. You're forever cutting it back and trying to control it, but it won't do your bidding. Notice, if you clear a piece of land to bare soil, what happens? Weeds grow. They hold the soil in place, preventing erosion, drying out and blowing away. You call those pioneer plants, first in the succession. Then, you get perennial weeds. Then, small bushes and different plants, next fruit trees maybe, their waste all the time building soil until some larger trees can establish themselves and eventually the giant broad leaves, maples, beeches, etc. Now, you might get enough trees to create a self-sustaining rain-forest, where so much moisture evaporates through the leaves of the plants (as much as 300 gallons a day from a large tree) that they create their own atmosphere above the forest, so laden with moisture that it falls back down as rain, and this cycle continues until someone or something, like a fire, destroys the mass that makes this happen. Think Amazon and Congo forests.

So, Our Nature undisturbed, does this, if you're a believer and consider this God's creation, you could conclude that this is God's will. If we keep cutting these forests down, are we against God's will, when in fact some pray, "may God's will be done?" From this, you could even say humans owe their existence to weeds, is that humbling!

Now, you have a kind of free will – which is also the will to destroy yourselves, (and Me) so you must use it carefully, otherwise, as is happening, you will destroy that which supports you. As you become more human, which many of you aren't, you may realize you don't have to kill biology to eat. You can maintain yourselves botanically. That's a quantum compassion step. "Thou shalt not kill" – so much! And if you do that correctly, you will even be healthier and possibly live longer. Does that interest any of you?

If God's will is expressed through Nature, can We say the Amazon and the Congo are that will, therefore to destroy them is inhuman will, whereby a human, if we equate humanness with closeness to God, should be in line with the will of God.

Instead of learning from the Native American tradition, that preserved the ecology of the Americas well into the 17th century - whereas the Middle East and Europe's ecology was trashed by 8,000 BCE. - the invading Christians, because of their deluded supremacy, had the audacity to forcefully educate indigenous people, all over the world. An education that backs up their system, praising their ways saying, "this is how technically advanced people live," maybe as a shield against a more egalitarian system that Jesus might promote. Is it possible to equate a trashed ecology – alienating us from Nature – with the root causes of modern society's violence?

You need a new modern lifestyle that is compatible with God's will and with Nature, in all its relationships: climate, biodiversity, ecological harmony, resource limits/balance, soil, water, air and marine life.

The hubris of the early European settlers in the Americas, led them to see the Native Americans as mentally inferior because they hadn't developed technological achievements, or the practice of large-scale agriculture. But these invading people had trashed their own ecology millennia before and so had to develop such things.

The Native Americans knew they were living in their food pantry and treated it with so much care and respect that it was still supportive of their lives, so they didn't need steel and weapons of mass destruction and ploughs.

What you see in the U.S. today is a desert compared to pre-invasion. The abundance that the invaders encountered was immediately exploited, sold, transported elsewhere, and trashed. The indigenous people, watching this unfold, must have thought they were watching the devil's children, not the so-called followers of a non-materialistic prophet, like Jesus. How many more wild fires will it take, even now, to change their course? The reckoning may be nigh, as they would say!

25. No Expectations:

I have no expectation that you will do any of this.

Your experts have already observed that 70% of My insect population has disappeared. Ask yourself, when will the locusts start flying over the horizon and consuming all plant matter? Even I don't know. Is it 80% insect loss, 85 or 90%? You'll drag out the old 'God's wrath' again when it happens. But now you see it was always you trashing the ecology of your regions, pushing My tipping points to their limit, now reaching the limit of 'more.' Incidentally, there's a lot of people standing in the wings who haven't reached a high level of consumption yet, and they're 'dying' to join you.

Neither you nor I are the final arbiters of what happens. You have set so many things in motion. But as the poet, Omar Khayyam said: "The moving finger writes; and, having writ, moves on: nor all your piety nor wit shall lure it back to cancel half a line, nor all your tears wash out a word of it."

WRAP UP:

This is a basic-needs, wholistic introductory explanation, perhaps to set people on their sustainability, self-reliant, regenerative journey. So much more can be done or conceived if we all set our minds to the task. Be a first adopter/responder. Amaze us. Let's build an alternative to fragile modernism and take some control of the important things in our life. Let us get re-acquainted with Nature – big time and heal our subconscious eco-trauma. If you find the WHYS in part 2 difficult, start a reading group and study together. If you share these difficult realizations with others, don't break their legs and leave – give the antidote and action items also. This is a call to action while there is still an abundance. I think, if you study this book, you'll have begun the journey of a sustainability, self-reliant, regenerative designer, who can then inspire others.

And just a reminder, that although the universe is a wonder, ultimately it is an electromagnetic fiction; so always return to the uncreated, eternal part of you at the center of your being when it all becomes overwhelming, and seek solace there.

FURTHER READING/RESOURCES:

Just Enough – Azby Brown. Pre-industrial sustainable society with many lessons for today. It's very organic and agricultural, which industrial modernity may become, one day, except that there will be all these material resources left around everywhere – imagine how that society might look.

Retrosuburbia – David Holmgren. An amazing work. This could be said to be the definitive version of the content mentioned here. However, I applied many of these things on my own property years before its publication (featuring them at my YouTube channel:

https://www.youtube.com/tonyfixit).

So, I can't be accused of plagiarism, and many of you may not want a 600-page version of this, hence the word 'primer' in my title.

Designing Regenerative Cultures – Daniel Christian Wahl

Agricide: The Hidden Farm and Food Crises That Affects Us All, Michael W. Fox, 2nd Edition 1996

Thinking In Systems, A Primer – Donella H. Meadows

The Self-Sufficiency Garden – Huw Richards, Sam Cooper

The Forager's Garden – Anna Locke

How To Fall In Love With The Future - Rob Hopkins

The Diet/Climate Connection, radio documentary.
https://www.humanmedia.org/product/diet-climate-connection/

 Plants For A Future www.pfaf.org Great publications and free online resource

www.Permaculture.co.uk Permaculture magazine, UK published, available in some U.S. bookstores

About the author, Tony Buck

I'm concerned about the sustainability of our age. I've had various work experience in my tender 74 years. I didn't get to university as my parents didn't value it. So, I ended up doing a five-year apprenticeship as a Toolmaker/machinist with a Rolls Royce company, mainly working in aerospace. I finished that at 21; and being bored and desiring some kind of adventure, I then travelled overland extensively through my twenties: Europe, Africa from north to south, USA, Central America, Sri Lanka and India, sometimes working in engineering environments. From 30 onward I've mainly been self-employed in the home improvement field, taking a few side roads into radio documentary production, a two-year TV co-host on the Discovery channel program, Gimme Shelter; and the publishing industry. I'm a lifelong learner. And because I've spent most of my life as a problem solver, that pattern is ingrained in me. Also, a lifelong edible gardener and exploration into herbal remedies, which led to becoming a Penn State Master Gardener and doing a Permaculture Design Certificate, incorporating both into my practices. And, now, becoming deeply aware about the state of our world and the problems we're going to face, my brain went into problem solving mode, giving birth to FSN.

INDEX:

A
Agricide 50
Agriculture/pharmaceutical complex 74
Air-chimney-effect 13
Air conditioning 83
Africa 13
Amory Lovins 4, 80,
Antibiotic overuse 76
Azby Brown 4

B
Batteries: community size   9, Lithium Iron Phosphate 8, Thermal 9,
Beavers 60
Bees 26
Benjamin Rush, Dr., 30, 77,
Berm 45
Bill Molison 4
Bioproductivity 58

C
Children in Permaculture Manual 80
Crafts 54
Crisis mega and poly 4
Cleveland Clinic 74
Compost 36
Contour 'A' frame 45

Council on Clean Transportation report 81
Covid Pandemic 64, 75,

D
Daniel Wahl 58
David Holmgren 4
Delaware Valley 6 , DVRPC food study 22,
De-witched 64
Donella Meadows 57, 66, 79,
Doug Tallamay, Prof. 38

E
Earth-Systems 4
Economic: Basic needs economy   64, household 52, self-preservation 17,
Ecosystems functions 58
Electromagnetic fiction 85
Emergy 51
Energy, household, know, energy assessments, conserve, R40 walls, 6 – 10

F
Feed in tariff 8
Fernand Braudel 65
Food animals 39

Forced air system 6
Foundation for Ecological Economics 71
Francisco Varela 48
Frost vs. Freezing 24

G
Gardening: styles, roof growing, wicking planters, nature in, plant fertilizer 22 – 41
Gatherer/hunter 60
Geoff Lawton 33
Geoffrey West, Physicist 61
Geothermal furnace 6, industrial scale 9,
Global Alliance for the Future of Food 49
God: sky God 62, God's will 84, wrath 85,
Great recession 70

H
Haber/Bosch process 74
Heat pump 6
Hentrepreneurs 52
Herbs 31
Household economy 52
Howard T. Odum 51, 55,
Hugleculture 36

I
Indigenous people 60
IPES reports 65, 71,

J
Jane Jacobs: transactions of decline 15, import substitution 51,
John Robbins 75
Joseph Tainter, Prof. 49

K
Kate Raworth, doughnut economics 70
Ken Robinson 78

L
Life Saver jerry can 46
Limits to Growth book 71, 83,

M
Mark Hyman, MD. quotes: 23, 49, 75,
Mark of a slave 69
Mega-crisis 4
Melanie Joy, PhD. 76
Mid-Atlantic region 6

N
Nate Hagens 51
National Academies workshop quote 77
National Geographic Society 74
National Rural Health Association 71
Nuclear 13

P
Paul Chatterton 81
Permaculture principles 59
Planetary Boundaries 60
Planned obsolescence 65
Plant families 29
Poly-crisis 4
Project Drawdown 82

R
Rainwater harvesting 44, Specs. 44, A-frame 45, ground water 47,
Regional conflict 63
Renewable energy: solar 8, wind turbine 10, woodstove 10
Repair Cafes 67
Richard Louv 79
Rob Hopkins 4
Root cellar 11

S
Sally Bingham 84
Sardinia 6
Sky water 1
Solar photovoltaic panels 8, solar hydronic panels 8,
Steve Solomon 28
Spring-house 11
Succession 41

Sun angle   15
Sun penetrable structures   16
Sustainable: age   18,   authentic   69,   sustain-in-place   4,

T
TEEBAgFood report   73
Thermal storage heater   9
Tipping points   62
Transition Town   19
Turtle Island   60,   Natives   60,

U
Unintended consequence   4
Universities: Uni of Illinois   29, Penn State   39,
U.N. SDGs   73, Food and Ag Organization   82,
USDA report   72,   73,
Utopianism for a Dying Planet   68

W
World Economic Forum   70

Z
Zoonotic disease   75
Zone: in the house   17, in the garden   24,

www.ingramcontent.com/pod-product-compliance
Lightning Source LLC
Chambersburg PA
CBHW080447110426
42743CB00016B/3303